Reactive Patterns with RxJS for Angular

A practical guide to managing your Angular application's data reactively and efficiently using RxJS 7

Lamis Chebbi

BIRMINGHAM—MUMBAI

Reactive Patterns with RxJS for Angular

Associate Group Product Manager: Pavan Ramchandani

Publishing Product Manager: Ashitosh Gupta

Senior Editor: Mark Dsouza

Content Development Editor: Divya Vijayan

Technical Editor: Shubham Sharma

Copy Editor: Safis Editing

Project Coordinator: Ajesh Devavaram

Proofreader: Safis Editing

Indexer: Rekha Nair

Production Designer: Alishon Mendonca

Marketing Coordinator: Elizabeth Varghese

First published: April 2022

Production reference: 2210422

Published by Packt Publishing Ltd.

Livery Place

35 Livery Street

Birmingham

B3 2PB, UK.

ISBN 978-1-80181-151-4

www.packt.com

To my father, who taught me diligence, perseverance, and work ethic. Thank you for always being there to support me and lift me up.

To my mother, who taught me selflessness and doing things with love. Thank you for your enduring encouragement during the writing of this book.

To my brother and my sisters, for their continuous support.

-Lamis Chebbi

Contributors

About the author

Lamis Chebbi is a Google Developer Expert for Angular and an Auth0 ambassador.

She is an enthusiastic software engineer with a strong passion for the modern web. She's the founder of Angular Tunisia, a member of the WWCode community, a speaker, a content creator, and a trainer. She has been into Angular for the past few years and loves to share her knowledge about Angular through participating in workshops and organizing training sessions. ng-girls is one of the communities she supports. Empowering women and students is one of her highest priorities. Besides Angular and the web, Lamis loves music, traveling, chromotherapy, and volunteering. Last but not least, she's a forever student.

I want to thank all the people that believed in me and supported me.

I am thankful for the people who helped me in the journey.

I am thankful for the people who inspired me in the journey.

About the reviewer

Dave Muellerchen is a freelancer. He loves sharing his self-taught knowledge of JavaScript at meetups and conferences.

His passion for communities shows in his commitment to them. He is the organizer of the Angular Hamburg Meetup and Tech Meetup Hamburg. He is also a team member at the Angular conference in Germany (ng-de) and a Google Developer Expert for web technologies. He streams developer content on Twitch.

Thanks to my wife, who has my back to do what I do. Thank you my sons, for the fun and the distraction. And of course, thank you Lamis for your trust.

Anu Nagan G has worked in various corporate organizations starting from SaaS startup [GenDeep], midsize [GAVS], Fortune 500 companies [DXC] playing various roles there such as Technical Product Manager, Full Stack Product Lead [Angular, Java, Python, AWS], Delivery Lead respectively in his 8 years of tenure. Currently, he is with Bounteous, leading parallel projects such as Clinical mobile app development, Fintech marketing data migration. Contributed to various AIOps products ZIF, Gcare in the past. He is an avid reader, cinephile, who loves to play Guitar, makes short films with his friends.

I would like to dedicate this to my grandparents who are celebrating their 82nd anniversary, to my wife and we are expecting. Happy birthday Hema.

Table of Contents

3
A Walkthrough of the Application

Part 2 – A Trip into Reactive Patterns

4
Fetching Data as Streams

5
Error Handling

6

Combining Streams

7

Transforming Streams

Part 3 – Multicasting Takes You to New Places

8

Multicasting Essentials

9

Caching Streams

10

Sharing Data between Components

11

Bulk Operations

12
Processing Real-Time Updates

Part 4 – Final Touch

13
Testing RxJS Observables

Preface

Switching to a reactive mindset is one of the biggest challenges when you start learning Reactive programming using RxJS. I believe that the reactive mindset is gradually achieved by learning reactive patterns and comparing the reactive way with the imperative one to distinguish the difference and the benefits.

That's why I wrote this book, which gathers a set of reactive patterns applied in an Angular application. Learning reactive patterns helps with managing your application's data efficiently, writing clean and maintainable code, reacting to user changes faster, and consequently, enhancing the user experience.

So, all that you have to do is get started!

Who this book is for

The book is for Angular developers who want to use RxJS to build reactive web applications. This book assumes beginner-level knowledge of and experience with Angular, RxJS, TypeScript, and functional programming concepts.

What this book covers

Chapter 1, The Power of the Reactive Paradigm, explains the fundamentals of Reactive programming.

Chapter 2, RxJS 7 – The Major Features, focuses on the main improvements of RxJS 7.

Chapter 3, A Walkthrough of the Application, highlights the architecture and requirements of the application that we will be building gradually.

Chapter 4, Fetching Data as Streams, explains the first reactive pattern for fetching data.

Chapter 5, Error Handling, details the error handling strategies and the reactive patterns for handling errors.

Chapter 6, Combining Streams, explains the reactive pattern for combining streams.

Chapter 7, Transforming Streams, explains the reactive pattern for transforming streams.

Chapter 8, Multicasting Essentials, focuses on the multicasting approach essentials.

Chapter 9, Caching Streams, explains the reactive pattern for caching streams.

Chapter 10, Sharing Data between Components, explains the reactive patterns for sharing data between components.

Chapter 11, Bulk Operations, explores the reactive pattern for performing bulk actions.

Chapter 12, Processing Real-Time Updates, explores the reactive pattern for consuming real-time updates.

Chapter 13, Testing RxJS Observables, explains the different strategies for testing reactive patterns.

To get the most out of this book

All code examples have been tested using Angular 12 on a Windows operating system. However, it should work with future releases too.

Software/hardware covered in the book	Operating system requirements
Angular 12 and above	Windows, macOS, or Linux
TypeScript 4.3.2 and above	Windows, macOS, or Linux
RxJS 7 and above	Windows, macOS, or Linux
primeng 12 and above	Windows, macOS, or Linux
Bootstrap 3.37 and above	Windows, macOS, or Linux

Please make sure you follow the prerequisites at `https://angular.io/guide/setup-local`. The prerequisites include the environment setup and the technologies needed in order to install and use Angular.

We also used the Bootstrap library to manage the application responsiveness. We used primeng as a library of rich components and RxJS 7 as the reactive library, of course.

If you are using the digital version of this book, we advise you to type the code yourself or access the code from the book's GitHub repository (a link is available in the next section). Doing so will help you avoid any potential errors related to the copying and pasting of code.

Download the example code files

You can download the example code files for this book from GitHub at `https://github.com/PacktPublishing/Reactive-Patterns-with-RxJS-for-Angular`. If there's an update to the code, it will be updated in the GitHub repository.

We also have other code bundles from our rich catalog of books and videos available at `https://github.com/PacktPublishing/`. Check them out!

Download the color images

We also provide a PDF file that has color images of the screenshots and diagrams used in this book. You can download it here: `https://static.packt-cdn.com/downloads/9781801811514_ColorImages.pdf`.

Conventions used

There are a number of text conventions used throughout this book.

`Code in text`: Indicates code words in text, database table names, folder names, filenames, file extensions, pathnames, dummy URLs, user input, and Twitter handles. Here is an example: "In the `try` block, you place your risky statements, and inside `catch`, you handle the possible exceptions."

A block of code is set as follows:

```
behaviourSubject$.subscribe({
  next: (message) => console.log(message),
  error: (error) => console.log(error),
  complete: () => console.log('Stream Completed'),
});
```

When we wish to draw your attention to a particular part of a code block, the relevant lines or items are set in bold:

```
behaviourSubject$.subscribe({
  next: (message) => console.log(message),
  error: (error) => console.log(error),
  complete: () => console.log('Stream Completed'),
});
```

Any command-line input or output is written as follows:

```
$ mkdir css
$ cd css
```

Bold: Indicates a new term, an important word, or words that you see onscreen. For instance, words in menus or dialog boxes appear in **bold**. Here is an example: "Select **System info** from the **Administration** panel."

> **Tips or Important Notes**
> Appear like this.

Get in touch

Feedback from our readers is always welcome.

General feedback: If you have questions about any aspect of this book, email us at customercare@packtpub.com and mention the book title in the subject of your message.

Errata: Although we have taken every care to ensure the accuracy of our content, mistakes do happen. If you have found a mistake in this book, we would be grateful if you would report this to us. Please visit www.packtpub.com/support/errata and fill in the form.

Piracy: If you come across any illegal copies of our works in any form on the internet, we would be grateful if you would provide us with the location address or website name. Please contact us at copyright@packt.com with a link to the material.

If you are interested in becoming an author: If there is a topic that you have expertise in and you are interested in either writing or contributing to a book, please visit authors.packtpub.com.

Share Your Thoughts

Once you've read *Reactive Patterns with RxJS for Angular*, we'd love to hear your thoughts! Scan the QR code below to go straight to the Amazon review page for this book and share your feedback.

https://packt.link/r/1801811512

Your review is important to us and the tech community and will help us make sure we're delivering excellent quality content.

Part 1 – Introduction

In this section, you will understand the importance of using the reactive paradigm in an Angular application, as well as the new features of RxJS 7. In the third chapter, we will introduce the application that we are going to progressively build as we go through the book.

This part comprises the following chapters:

- *Chapter 1, The Power of the Reactive Paradigm*
- *Chapter 2, RxJS 7 – The Major Features*
- *Chapter 3, A Walkthrough of the Application*

1
The Power of the Reactive Paradigm

This book is based entirely on useful reactive patterns in Angular applications. Reactive patterns are reusable solutions to a commonly occurring problem using reactive programming. Behind all of these patterns, there is a new way of thinking, new architecture, new coding styles, and new tools.

I know you are impatient to write your first reactive pattern in Angular, but before doing that, and to help you take full advantage of all the RxJS patterns and leverage the reactive paradigm, we will start by explaining, in detail, all the fundamentals. Additionally, we will prepare the groundwork for the following chapters. First, let's start with a basic understanding of the reactive paradigm, its advantages, and the problems it solves. And best of all, let's get into the reactive mindset and start thinking reactively.

We will begin by highlighting the pillars and the advantages of the reactive paradigm. Then, we will describe the relationship between Angular and RxJS. Finally, we will explain the **Marble diagram** and why it is useful.

Giving an insight into the fundamentals of the reactive paradigm is incredibly important. This will ensure you get the basics right, help you understand the usefulness of the reactive approach, and consequently, help you determine which situation it is best to use it in.

In this chapter, we're going to cover the following topics:

- Exploring the pillars of reactive programming
- Using RxJS in Angular and its advantages
- Learning about the marble diagram – our secret weapon

Technical requirements

This chapter does not require an environment setup or installation steps. All the code snippets here are just examples to illustrate the concepts. This book assumes that you have a basic understanding of Angular and RxJS.

Exploring the pillars of reactive programming

Let's begin with a little bit of background!

Reactive programming is among the major programming paradigms used by developers worldwide. Every programming paradigm solves some problems and has its own advantages. By definition, reactive programming is programming with asynchronous data streams and is based on observer patterns. So, let's talk about these pillars of reactive programming!

Data streams

Data streams are the spine of reactive programming. Everything that might change or happen over time (you don't know when exactly) is represented as a stream, such as data, events, notifications, and messages. Reactive programming is about reacting to changes as soon as they are emitted!

An excellent example of data streams is UI events. Let's suppose that we have an HTML button, and we want to execute an action whenever a user clicks on it. Here, we can think of the click event as a stream:

```
//HTML code
<button id='save'>Save</button>
```

```
//TS code
const saveElement = document.getElementById('save');
saveElement.addEventListener('click', processClick);
```

```
function processClick(event) {
    console.log('Hi');
}
```

As implemented in the preceding code snippet, in order to react to this click event, we register an EventListener event. Then, every time a click occurs, the processClick method is called to execute a side effect. In our case, we are just logging Hi in the console.

As you might have gathered, to be able to react when something happens and execute a side effect, you should listen to the streams to become notified. We can say *listen* or observe to get closer to the reactive terminology. And this leads us to the *observer* design pattern, which is at the heart of reactive programming.

Observer patterns

The observer pattern is based on two main roles: a publisher and a subscriber.

A publisher maintains a list of subscribers and notifies them or propagates a change every time there is an update. On the other hand, a subscriber performs an update or executes a side effect every time they receive a notification from the publisher:

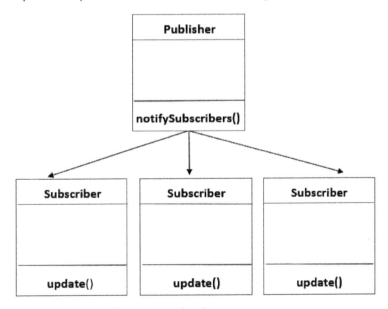

Figure 1.1 – The observer pattern

So, to get notified about any updates, you need to subscribe to the publisher. A real-world analogy would be a newsletter; you don't get any emails if you don't subscribe to a newsletter.

This leads us to the building blocks of RxJS. They include the following:

- **Observables**: These are a representation of the data streams that notify the observers of any change.

- **Observers**: These are the consumers of the data streams emitted by observables.

RxJS combines the observer pattern with the iterator pattern and functional programming to process and handle asynchronous events.

This was a reminder of the fundamentals of reactive programming. Remember, it is crucial to understand when to put a reactive implementation in place and when to avoid it.

In general, whenever you have to handle asynchronous tasks in your Angular application, always think of RxJS. The main advantages of RxJS over other asynchronous APIs are listed as follows:

- RxJS makes dealing with event-based programs, asynchronous data calls, and callbacks an easy task.

- Observables guarantee consistency. They emit multiple values over time so that you can consume continuous data streams.

- Observables are lazy; they are not executed until you subscribe to them. This helps with writing declarative code that is clean, efficient, and easy to understand and maintain.

- Observables can be canceled, completed, and retrieved at any moment. This makes a lot of sense in many real-world scenarios.

- RxJS provides many operators with a functional style to manipulate collections and optimize side effects.

- Observables push errors to the subscribers and provide a clean way to handle errors.

- RxJS allows you to write clean and efficient code to handle asynchronous data in your application.

Now that we have given some insight into the reactive programming pillars and detailed the major advantages of RxJS, let's shed some light on the relationship between Angular and RxJS.

Using RxJS in Angular and its advantages

RxJS is a first-class citizen in Angular. It is part of the Angular ecosystem and is used in many features to handle asynchronous operations. Primarily, this includes the following:

- **HTTP client module**
- **Router module**
- **Reactive forms**
- **Event emitter**
- **Async pipe**

We will discuss each of the following concepts in the subsequent subsections.

> **Note**
>
> We recommend taking a quick look at `https://angular.io/docs`. Here, you can find further details about the features mentioned earlier.

The HTTP client module

You might be familiar with the HTTP client API provided by Angular in order to communicate with your server over the HTTP protocol. The HttpClient service is based on observables to manage all transactions. This means that the result of calling the API methods (such as GET, PATCH, POST, or PUT) is an observable.

In the following code snippet, we have an example of an Angular service that injects the HttpClient service and fetches data from the server using the HttpClient. get() method:

```
Import { Injectable } from '@angular/core';
import { HttpClient } from '@angular/common/http';
import { Observable} from 'rxjs';
import { environment } from '@env/environment';
const BASE_PATH = environment.basePath;


@Injectable()
export class RecipesService {
constructor(private http: HttpClient) { }
getRecipes(): Observable<Recipe[]> {
return this.http.get<Recipe[]>(`${BASE_PATH}/recipes/search/
```

```
all`);
}
```

The following is the content of the `environment.ts` file where we define the `basePath` property of our backend:

```
export const environment = {
  basePath: '/app/rest',
  production: false
};
```

The `getRecipes()` method or, to be more accurate, the call to `this.http.get<Recipe>(`${BASE_PATH}/recipes/search`)` returns an observable that you should subscribe to in order to issue the `GET` request to the server. Please note that this is an example of an HTTP transaction, and it is the same for all of the other HTTP methods available in the API (such as `POST`, `PUT`, and `PATCH`)

For those familiar with promise-based HTTP APIs, you might be wondering, in this case, what the advantages of using observables are.

Well, there are a lot of advantages but the most important ones are listed as follows:

- Observables are cancellable, so you can cancel the HTTP request whenever you want by calling the unsubscribe method.

- Also, you can retry HTTP requests when an error occurs or an exception is thrown.

- The server's response cannot be mutated by observables, although this can be the case when chaining `then()` to promises.

The router module

The router module, which is available in the `@angular/router` package, uses observables in router events and activated routes.

Router events

The router exposes events as observables. The router events allow you to intercept the navigation life cycle. The following list shows the sequence of router events:

- `NavigationStart`
- `RouteConfigLoadStart`
- `RouteConfigLoadEnd`

- RoutesRecognized

- GuardsCheckStart

- ChildActivationStart

- ActivationStart

- GuardsCheckEnd

- ResolveStart

- ResolveEnd

- ActivationEnd

- ChildActivationEnd

- NavigationEnd

- NavigationCancel

- NavigationError

- Scroll

> **Note**
>
> We recommend that you take a quick look at `https://angular.io/api/router/Event`. Here, you can find further details about the events and their order.

To intercept all the events that the router goes through, first, you should inject the `Router` service, which provides navigation and URL manipulation capabilities. Then, subscribe to the `events` observable available in the `Router` object, and filter the events of the `RouterEvent` type using the `rxjs` filter operator.

This is an example of an Angular service that injects the `Router` object in the constructor, subscribes to the router events, and just traces the event ID and path in the console. However, note that you can also introduce pretty much any specific behavior:

```
import { Injectable } from '@angular/core';
import { Router, RouterEvent } from '@angular/router';
import { filter } from 'rxjs/operators';
@Injectable()
export class CustomRouteService {
  constructor(public router: Router) {
    this.router.events.pipe(
```

```
      filter(event => event instanceof RouterEvent)
    ).subscribe((event: RouterEvent) => {
      console.log(`The current event is : ${event.id} |
              event.url`);
    });
  }
}
```

You can filter any specific event by putting the target type. The following code example only filters the NavigationStart event and traces the event ID and path inside the console. However, you can also introduce pretty much any specific behavior:

```
import { Injectable } from '@angular/core';
import { NavigationStart, Router } from '@angular/router';
import { filter } from 'rxjs/operators';

@Injectable()
export class CustomRouteService {
  constructor(public router: Router) {
    this.router.events.pipe(
        filter(event => event instanceof NavigationStart)
    ).subscribe((event: NavigationStart) => {
      console.log(`The current event is : ${event.id} |
              event.url`);
    });

  }
}
```

The majority of Angular applications have a routing mechanism. The router events change frequently over time, and it makes sense to listen to changes to execute the side effects. That's why observables are a flexible way in which to handle those streams.

The activated route

The `ActivatedRoute` class is a router service that you can inject into your components to retrieve information about a route's path and parameters. Many properties are based on observables. Here, you will find the contract (refers to the exposed methods and properties) of the activated route class:

```
class ActivatedRoute {
  snapshot: ActivatedRouteSnapshot
  url: Observable<UrlSegment[]>
  params: Observable<Params>
  queryParams: Observable<Params>
  fragment: Observable<string | null>
  data: Observable<Data>
  outlet: string
  component: Type<any> | string | null
  routeConfig: Route | null
  root: ActivatedRoute
  parent: ActivatedRoute | null
  firstChild: ActivatedRoute | null
  children: ActivatedRoute[]
  pathFromRoot: ActivatedRoute[]
  paramMap: Observable<ParamMap>
  queryParamMap: Observable<ParamMap>
  toString(): string
}
```

As you might have gathered, `url`, `params`, `queryParams`, `fragment`, `data`, `paramMap`, and `queryParamMap` are represented as observables. Refer to the following list:

- `url`: This is an observable that holds the URL of the active route.

- `params`: This is an observable that holds the parameters of the active route.

- `queryParams`: This is an observable that holds the query parameters shared by all of the routes.

- `fragment`: This is an observable that holds the URL fragment shared by all the routes.

- `data`: This is an observable that holds the static and resolved data of the active route.

- `paramMap`: This is an observable that holds a map of the required parameters and the optional parameters of the active route.

- `queryParamMap`: This is an observable that holds a map of the query parameters available to all the routes.

All these parameters might change over time. Routes might share parameters, the parameters might have dynamic values, and it makes perfect sense to listen to those changes to register side effects or update the list of parameters.

Here's an example of an Angular component that injects the `ActivatedRoute` class in the constructor and subscribes, in the `ngOnInit()` method, to the following:

- The `url` property of `activatedRoute`, logging the URL in the console

- The `queryParams` property of `activatedRoute` in order to retrieve the parameter *criteria* and store it in a local property, named `criteria`:

```
import { Component, OnInit } from '@angular/core';
import { ActivatedRoute } from '@angular/router';


@Component({
   selector: 'app-recipes',
   templateUrl: './recipes.component.html'
})
export class RecipesComponent implements OnInit {
   criteria: any;
   constructor(private activatedRoute: ActivatedRoute)
   { }

   ngOnInit() {
     this.activatedRoute.url
       .subscribe(url => console.log('The URL changed
                                     to: ' + url));

     this.activatedRoute.queryParams.subscribe(params
     => {
       this.processCriteria(params.criteria);
```

```
        });
    }
    processCriteria(criteria: any) {
        this.criteria = criteria;
    }
}
```

Reactive forms

Reactive forms available under the `@angular/forms` package are based on observables to track form control changes. Here's the contract of the `FormControl` class in Angular:

```
class FormControl extends AbstractControl {
  //other properties here
  valueChanges: Observable<any>
  statusChanges: Observable<any>
}
```

The `FormControl` properties of `valueChanges` and `statusChanges` are represented as observables that trigger change events. Subscribing to a `FormControl` value change is a way of triggering application logic within the `component` class.

Here's an example of an Angular component that subscribes to the `valueChanges` of a `FormControl` property called *rating* and simply traces the value through `console. log(value)`. In this way, each time, you will get the changed value as an output:

```
import { Component, OnInit } from '@angular/core';
import { FormGroup } from '@angular/forms';

@Component({
  selector: 'app-recipes',
  templateUrl: './recipes.component.html'
})
export class MyComponent implements OnInit {
  form!: FormGroup;

  ngOnInit() {
    const ratingControl = this.form.get('rating');
    ratingControl?.valueChanges.subscribe(
```

```
        (value) => {
            console.log(value);
        }
    );
  }
}
```

The event emitter

The event emitter, which is part of the @angular/core package, is used to emit data from a child component to a parent component through the @Output() decorator. The EventEmitter class extends the RxJS subject and registers handlers for events emitted by this instance:

```
class EventEmitter<T> extends Subject {
    constructor(isAsync?: boolean): EventEmitter<T>
    emit(value?: T): void
    subscribe(next?: (value: T) => void, error?: (error: any)
    => void, complete?: () => void): Subscription
}
```

This is what happens under the hood when you create an event emitter and emit a value.

The following is an example of an Angular component that emits the updated value of a recipe rating:

```
import { Component, Output } from '@angular/core';
import { EventEmitter } from 'events';

@Component({
    selector: 'app-recipes',
    templateUrl: './recipes.component.html'
})
export class RecipesComponent {
    constructor() {}
    @Output() updateRating = new EventEmitter();

    updateRecipe(value: string) {
        this.updateRating.emit(value);
```

```
    }
  }
```

The async pipe

Here, `AsyncPipe` automatically subscribes to an observable when used in a component's template and emits the latest value each time. This avoids subscribing logic in the component and helps with binding and updating your asynchronous streams data in the template. In this example, we are using an async pipe inside `ngIf`. This `div` tag will only be rendered when the `data$` variable emits something:

```
<div *ngIf="data$ | async"></div>
```

We will cover the advantages and usage of async pipes in *Chapter 4, Fetching Data as Streams*.

> **Note**
>
> In the previous code snippets, the subscription to the observables was done explicitly for demonstration purposes. In a real-world example, we should include the unsubscription logic if we use an explicit subscription. We will shed light on this in *Chapter 4, Fetching Data as Streams*.

Now that we have learned about the advantages of using RxJS in Angular and how it makes dealing with some concepts smoother, let's explore the marble diagram, which is very handy for understanding and visualizing the observable execution.

Learning about the marble diagram – our secret weapon

RxJS ships with more than 100 **operators**. Operators are one of the building blocks of RxJS. They are very useful for manipulating streams. All the reactive patterns that will be detailed later in this book are based on operators. And when it comes to explaining operators, it is better to refer to a visual representation. And that's why there are marble diagrams. Thankfully!

Marble diagrams are a visual representation of the operator's execution. We will be using the marble diagram in all chapters to understand the behavior of RxJS operators. At first, it might seem daunting, but it is delightfully simple. First, you only have to understand the anatomy of the diagram and then you're good to read and translate it. You will be able to understand any RxJS operator – those used in this book along with others, too.

So as we said, marble diagrams represent the execution of an operator. So, every diagram will include the following:

- **Input Observable(s)**: This represents one or many observables given as input to the operator.

- **Operator**: This represents the operator to be executed with its parameters.

- **Output Observable**: This represents the observable produced after the operator's execution:

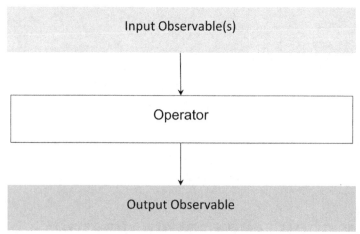

Figure 1.2 – The operator execution

Well, this is the big picture. Now, let's zoom in on the representation of the input/output observables. It includes the following:

- **The timeline**: Observables are asynchronous streams that produce data over time. Therefore, the representation of time is crucial in the marble diagram, and it is represented as an arrow flowing from left to right.

- **The marble values**: These are the values emitted by the observables over time.

- **The completion status**: The vertical line represents the successful completion of the observables.

- **The error status**: The X represents an error emitted by the observable. Neither values nor the vertical line representing the completion will be emitted thereafter:

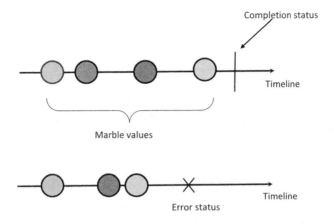

Figure 1.3 – Elements of the marble diagram

That's all the elements you need to know. Now, let's put all of the pieces together into a real marble diagram:

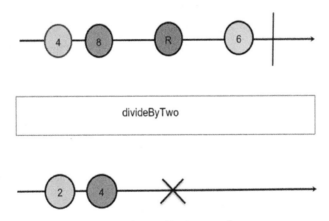

Figure 1.4 – An example of a marble diagram for a custom operator

Let's break down what is happening in the preceding diagram. As you might have guessed, we have a custom operator called `divideByTwo` that will emit half of every received number. When the input observable emits the values of 4 and 8, the output observable produces 2 and 4, respectively.

However, when the value of R, which is non-numeric, is emitted, then an error is thrown, indicating abnormal termination. This case is not handled in the operator code. The input observable continues the emission and then completes successfully. However, the value will never be processed because, after the error, the stream is closed.

At this level, we went through all of the elements composing the marble diagram. And you will be able to understand the operators used in the chapters to come.

Summary

In this chapter, we walked you through the fundamentals of reactive programming and which use cases it shines in. Then, we highlighted the use of reactive programming in Angular by illustrating concrete examples, implementations, and advantages. Finally, we explained the marble diagram, which will be our reference to explain RxJS operators in all the following chapters. In the next chapter, we will focus on RxJS 7's new features as we will be using this version of RxJS.

2
RxJS 7 – The Major Features

RxJS 7 was released on April 29, 2021. This new version came with a lot of improvements and new features over RxJS 6. Hence, we're going to use this version to benefit from the new features and guarantee optimized, high-quality code for our patterns. In this chapter, we will be discussing some of these features. We will only be covering certain features that we consider important and those that represent a major improvement over the features in RxJS 6.

We will begin this chapter by defining the bundle size and highlighting the importance of analyzing it. Then, we will compare the RxJS 6 and RxJS 7 bundles within an Angular app. After that, we will review some TypeScript typing improvements. Additionally, we will explain the reason behind the `toPromise()` deprecation and the newly offered alternatives. Finally, we will shed light on the API consistency improvements.

In this chapter, we're going to cover the following topics:

- Exploring the bundle size improvements
- Reviewing the TypeScript typing improvements
- Understanding the `toPromise()` deprecation
- Highlighting API consistency improvements

Technical requirements

This chapter does not require an environment setup or installation steps. All the code snippets here are just examples to illustrate the concepts. This book assumes that you have a basic understanding of Angular and RxJS.

Exploring the bundle size improvements

Every frontend application needs a number of JavaScript files to run. These files are either the ones you have written yourself or the external dependencies used to build your application, such as MomentJS, Lodash, or RxJS. A bundle is an output of a process that merges all of these files into a few (if not single) files in the most optimized way possible.

One of the major approaches commonly used to improve frontend performance is reducing the JavaScript bundle size. The smaller the size of the JavaScript bundle, the faster a page can load up the first time and be available to users.

The RxJS core team worked on reducing the bundle size of the library in version 7; they did a lot of refactoring to optimize the code and, consequently, the bundle size.

To get a better idea, let's measure the bundle sizes of two frontend applications using RxJS 6 and RxJS 7, respectively, and compare the size of the RxJS library in both applications. There are a lot of tools that can help you measure and analyze your bundles. The one that we are going to use is the **source map explorer**. The source map explorer enables you to analyze bundles that have a source map by offering a visual representation. In fact, it shows you an interactive tree map to help you determine where all the code is coming from, in addition to the size of the bundles that are emerging from both the external dependencies and the inner code.

The following figures represent the size of the RxJS 6 and RxJS 7 libraries within an Angular application, respectively. They have been captured using a generated source-map-explorer report.

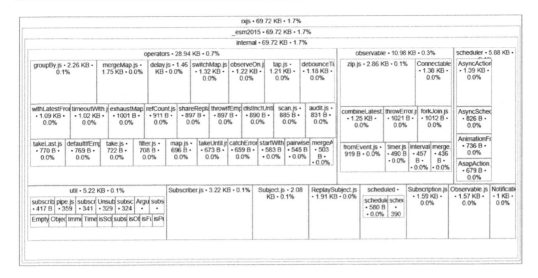

Figure 2.1 – The size of the RxJS 6 library in a medium Angular app

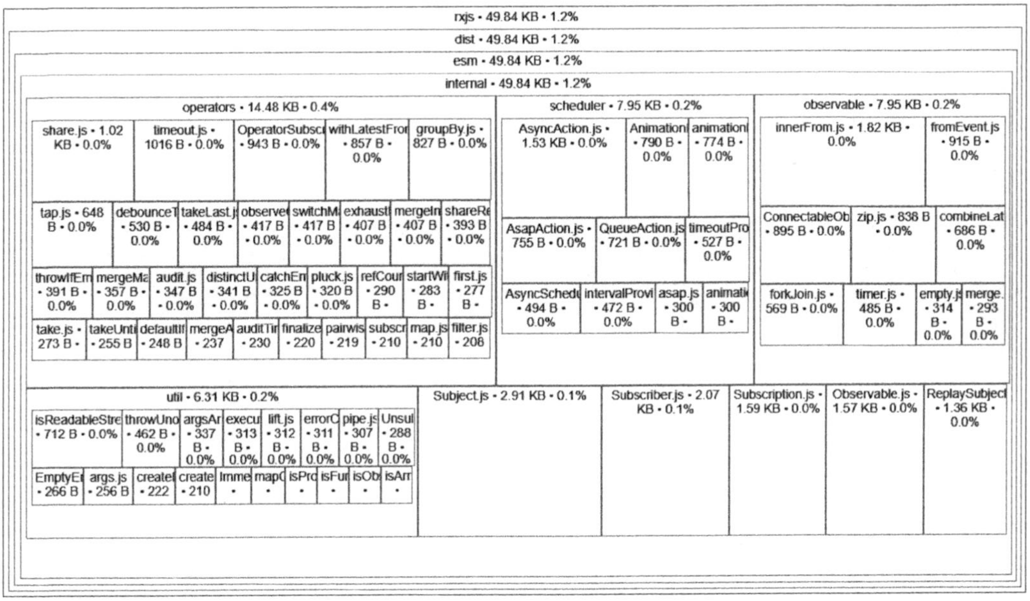

Figure 2.2 – The size of the RxJS 7 library in a medium Angular app

As you can see, after the migration from RxJS 6 to RxJS 7, the bundle size of the library dropped from 69.72 KB to 49.84 KB without affecting the written code.

These results are generated from a medium Angular app. The difference between the bundle sizes of the two versions is quite prominent in larger applications. The size really depends on the RxJS concepts used; that's why it is different from one app to another.

On the other hand, operators come at a smaller cost. If we include every operator in RxJS 6, the bundled size of the operators will be around 52 KB, and in RxJS 7, it will be around 19 KB, even though RxJS 7 has more operators than RxJS 6.

Now that we know that RxJS 7 can be used to build apps with lower bundle sizes compared to RxJS 6, let's look at some of the other improvements of RxJS 7.

Reviewing the TypeScript typing improvements

RxJS 7 requires **TypeScript 4.2** and takes advantage of its latest features. This helped the RxJS core team to improve the package types while making them stricter, more accurate, and more flexible. Providing better types can prevent runtime problems and any mismatched type confusion ahead of time.

For example, in RxJS 6, you can create a subject of a specific type and call next() without passing arguments; while, in RxJS 7, the same instruction will cause a compilation error because the subject's specified type has not been respected.

So, if you want to call next() without passing something to it, you need to make sure that your subject accepts void as a type:

```
//RxJs 6 example
const subject = new Subject<number>();
subject.next(); //compiles fine


//RxJS 7 example
const subject = new Subject<number>();
subject.next(); //compilation error


//RxJS 7 example
const subject = new Subject<void>();
subject.next();//compiles fine
```

This was an example of typing improvements in RxJS7, and there are others. Now, let's take a look at the toPromise() deprecation. We will start by giving a little bit of background. Then, we will explain the deprecation and the new alternatives.

Understanding the toPromise() deprecation

One of the major deprecations of RxJS 7 is the `toPromise()` deprecation. `toPromise()` will be deleted permanently after the release of RxJS 8. So, it is highly recommended that you avoid using `toPromise()` in your future developments.

Now, let's give a little bit of background to understand the reason behind this deprecation. It is important to understand the use case of `toPromise()`, why this particular method is available, and when to use it. Additionally, it is important to understand the incoherent behavior of this method in RxJS 6 in order to anticipate problems that might arise.

Promises are used by many developers nowadays, and there are thousands of promise-based libraries. A promise is an object that holds the result (or failure) of an asynchronous operation.

Promises have been available in JavaScript through third-party libraries such as jQuery. Additionally, ECMAScript 6 added built-in support to JavaScript for promises.

The common key point between observables and promises is that both objects could produce values over time. However, the major difference is that observables can produce none or more than one value, while promises only produce one value when resolved successfully.

The `toPromise()` method available in RxJS is a util method that is used to convert an Observable to a Promise. The `toPromise()` subscribes to the Observable and returns the last value emitted by this Observable.

In RxJS 6, when an error happens, `toPromise()` returns undefined. But this is not accurate!

That's because you cannot differentiate between the case where no value was emitted before completion of the observable and the case where an undefined value was emitted last.

Let's look at the first example in the following snippet. Here, `toPromise()` will return the last value emitted by the observable, which is `World`:

```
const source$ = new Observable<string>(observer => {
    observer.next('Hello');
    observer.next('World');
    observer.complete();
});
hello();
async function hello() {
```

```
    const value = await source$.toPromise();
    console.log(value);
}
//console output
//World
```

Now, let's change the preceding example and make the observable complete without returning any values. In this case, toPromise() will return undefined:

```
const source$ = new Observable<string>(observer => {
  observer.complete();
});
hello();
async function hello() {
    const value = await source$.toPromise();
    console.log(value);
}
//console output
//undefined
```

Now, let's make the observable return undefined as a value:

```
const source$ = new Observable<string>(observer => {
observer.next(undefined);
observer.complete();
});
hello();
async function hello() {
    const value = await source$.toPromise();
    console.log(value);
}
//console output
//undefined
```

In this particular case, you cannot differentiate between the two situations where no value was emitted before completion and an undefined value was emitted last. A promise is a guarantee that a value will eventually be emitted; otherwise, the promise will throw an error.

When converting an observable into a promise, you might want to select which value to pick – either the first value that has arrived or the last one. Sometimes, you won't want to wait until the observable is completed; you need the first value as it arrives.

This was a confusing behavior, but luckily, it has been changed with the arrival of RxJS 7.

- `toPromise()` is now deprecated in favor of `firstValueFrom()` and `lastValueFrom()`.

The firstValueFrom() method

This method converts an observable into a promise by subscribing to the observable (which is given as a parameter) and returns the first value emitted by this observable. The subscription will be released immediately after returning the value. Additionally, it will reject with an `EmptyError` error if the observable completes with no values emitted:

```
import { firstValueFrom, lastValueFrom } from 'rxjs';
const source$ = new Observable<string>(observer => {
  observer.next('Hello');
  observer.next('World');
  observer.complete();
});
hello();
async function hello() {
  const value = await firstValueFrom(source$);
  console.log(value);
}
//console output
//Hello
```

In the preceding code snippet, we created an observable called `source$` that emits two values, `Hello` and `World`, and then completes. Calling `firstValueFrom(source$)` in the `hello()` function will return the first value emitted by the observable, which is `Hello`, and then completes.

The lastValueFrom() method

This method returns the last value emitted by an observable after its completion.

Also, it will reject with an `EmptyError` error if the observable completes with no values emitted:

```
import { firstValueFrom, lastValueFrom } from 'rxjs';
const source$ = new Observable<string>(observer => {
  observer.next('Hello');
  observer.next('World');
  observer.complete();
});
hello();
async function hello() {
  const value = await lastValueFrom(source$);
  console.log(value);
}
//console output
//World
```

In the preceding code snippet, we created an observable called `source$` that emits two values, `Hello` and `World`, and then completes. Calling `lastValueFrom(source$)` in the `hello()` function will return the last value emitted by the observable after the completion, which is `World`.

Empty errors

Now, let's bring our attention to a scenario where the observable does not return any values at all. Calling `lastValueFrom()`, as illustrated in the following code snippet, or `firstValueFrom()` will throw an error with a default message of `no elements in sequence`:

```
import { lastValueFrom } from 'rxjs';
const source$ = new Observable<string>(observer => {
  observer.complete();
});
hello();
async function hello() {
  const value = await lastValueFrom(source$);
```

```
      console.log(value);
}
//console output
//Error: no elements in sequence
```

So, the default behavior, when there is no value, is to throw a specific kind of error: EmptyError. However, if you want to customize this behavior, you can use the defaultValue parameter. The defaultValue parameter will be used to resolve a promise when the observable completes without emitting a value:

```
Const source$ = new Observable<string>(observer => {
   observer.complete();
});
hello();
async function hello() {
   const value = await lastValueFrom(source$, {
                                 defaultValue: 'DEFAULT' });
   console.log(value);
}
//console output
//DEFAULT
```

> **Note**
>
> The lastValueFrom() method is recommended when you're sure an observable will complete. The firstValueFrom() method is recommended when you're sure an observable will emit at least one value or complete.

Well, this is all that you need to know about the toPromise() deprecation. It is time to move to the next improvement regarding API consistency.

Highlighting API consistency improvements

RxJS 7 also ships with a fix of some weird behavior in the library. Let's consider the example of a concat operator:

> *"Concat: Creates an output observable, which sequentially emits all values from the first given observable and then moves on to the next."*

Let's consider the following sample:

```
concat(
of(1).pipe(
    tap(() => console.log('tap 1')),
    delay(100),
    finalize(() => console.log('Finalize 1'))
    ),
    of(2).pipe(
    tap(() => console.log('tap 2')),
    delay(100),
    finalize(() => console.log('Finalize 2'))
    )
    )
    .subscribe(x => console.log(x));

//console output
tap 1
1
tap 2
Finalize 1
2
Finalize 2
```

As you might have gathered, the finalization takes place after we subscribe to the next observable in the chain. This means that RxJS 6 didn't wait for finalization before subscribing to the next observable. So, finalize doesn't happen in the correct order.

In RxJs 7, this behavior has been fixed to respect the proper order:

```
concat(
of(1).pipe(
    tap(() => console.log('tap 1')),
    delay(100),
    finalize(() => console.log('Finalize 1'))
    ),
    of(2).pipe(
    tap(() => console.log('tap 2')),
```

```
        delay(100),
        finalize(() => console.log('Finalize 2'))
        )
    )
    .subscribe(x => console.log(x));



//console output
tap 1
1
Finalize 1
tap 2
2
Finalize 2
```

In the same way, the `concat` operator was deprecated in RxJS7 and replaced with `concatWith`. It will be removed in v8. For further details, please refer to the official documentation at `https://rxjs.dev/api/operators/concat`.

There are a lot of other improvements delivered in RxJS 7, namely, better memory usage as the majority of operators no longer retain outer values, a lot of bug fixes and documentation improvements, the consolidation of multicasting operators, renaming, and the deprecation of many operators.

We won't walk through all of those improvements as it is not the principal goal of this book. We can provide further details via the following official links:

- The changelog: `https://github.com/ReactiveX/rxjs/blob/master/CHANGELOG.md`

- The official documentation: `https://rxjs-dev.firebaseapp.com/6-to-7-change-summary`

Summary

In this chapter, we walked you through the main highlights of RxJS 7. We provided various categories of improvements with an example in each category. Now that we have got the basics right, it is time to start preparing and explaining the application that we are going to build in the next chapter, where we are going to implement all of the reactive patterns we have learned.

3

A Walkthrough of the Application

Now, we are one step closer to diving into reactive patterns, but before we do, let's explain in detail the app that we are going to build throughout this book that uses those patterns.

We will start by explaining the technical requirements followed by the user stories of the application. Furthermore, we will showcase an overview of the application interfaces and architecture. Last but not least, we will describe the components tree through a visual representation. By the end of this chapter, we will have all the required pieces in place to start implementing our application.

In this chapter, we're going to cover the following main topics:

- Our app's user stories
- Our app's architecture
- The components overview

Technical requirements

We are going to use **Angular 12** for our frontend. Version 12.1.1 of `@angular/cli` is used in this book. Please make sure you followed the prerequisites at `https://angular.io/guide/setup-local`. The prerequisites include the environment setup and the technologies needed in order to install and use Angular.

We are going to use version 7.5.4 of RxJS.

The front application uses the following dependencies:

- Bootstrap (version 3.3.7) – a toolkit for developing responsive web apps. For more details, please check out this official link: `https://getbootstrap.com/`.
- PrimeNG (version 12.0) – a rich library of open source native Angular UI components. For more details, please check out this official link: `https://primefaces.org/primeng/showcase/#/setup`.

Our app's user stories

As a food junkie, I wanted the application to be a book of recipes, allowing users and home cooks to browse and share delicious food recipes. The main aim of the app is to provide inspiration for meals as well as help users do the following:

- Share their recipes
- Save the favorite ones to easily find them
- Distinguish the top-rated recipes
- Filter out recipes according to some criteria

The app is composed of five interfaces, each of which will be discussed in the following subsections along with the landing page. Let's tackle these interfaces one by one.

View one – the landing page

This contains a list of available recipes, sorted according to popularity.

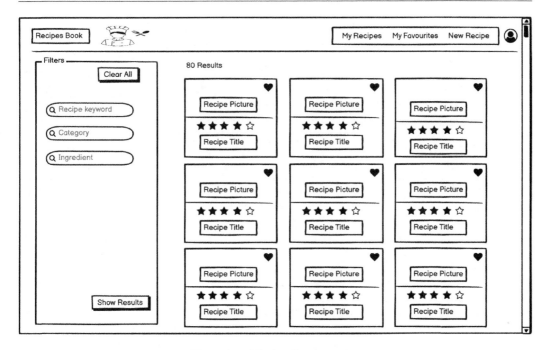

Figure 3.1 – The landing page view

In this view, users have the possibility to do the following:

- Quickly search for a recipe by setting filters according to multiple criteria (on the left-hand side)
- Clear the list of filters
- View the most popular recipes
- Rate the recipes by clicking on the number of stars
- Add a recipe to their favorites by clicking on the heart icon
- See a recipe's details by clicking on it
- View the total number of recipes

View two – the new recipe interface

This contains a form to create a new recipe.

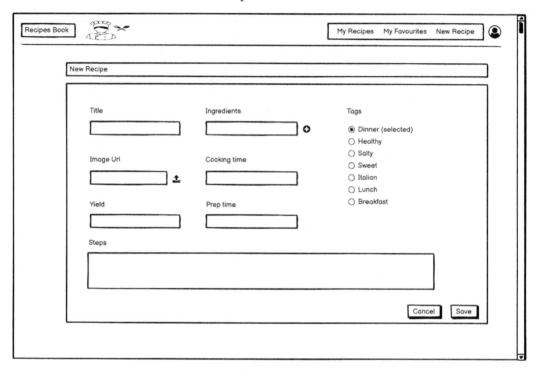

Figure 3.2 – The New Recipe view

In this view, users can create a new recipe by clicking on the **New Recipe** menu item located at the top right. A form containing the details of the recipe will be opened to fill out and save:

- **Title**: The title of the recipe
- **Ingredients**: The ingredients required to prepare the recipe
- **Image Url**: A good image of the meal prepared
- **Cooking time**: The time required to cook the meal
- **Yield**: The number of people that can be served by this meal

- **Prep time**: The time required to prepare the meal

- **Tags**: Key tags describing the recipe

- **Steps**: The steps required to prepare and cook the meal

View three – the My Recipes interface

This contains a list of recipes created by the user. They can edit and remove recipes by clicking on the edit and delete icons, respectively.

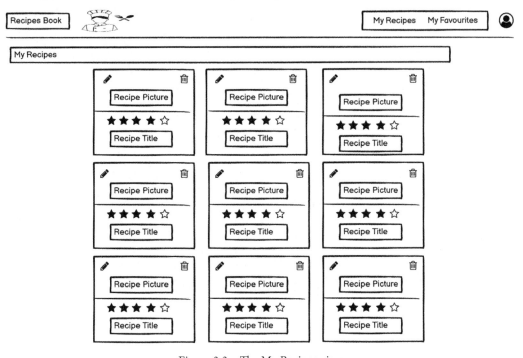

Figure 3.3 – The My Recipes view

View four – the My Favourites interface

This contains a list of the user's favorite recipes.

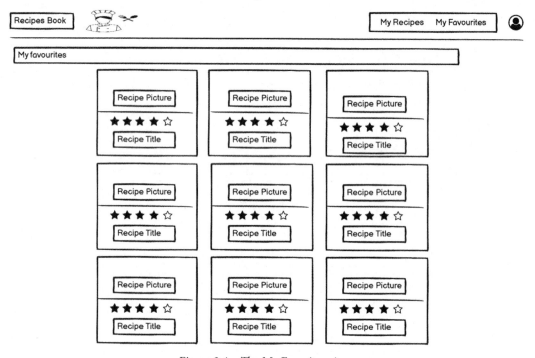

Figure 3.4 – The My Favorites view

View five – the modify recipe interface

This contains a form to edit an existing recipe.

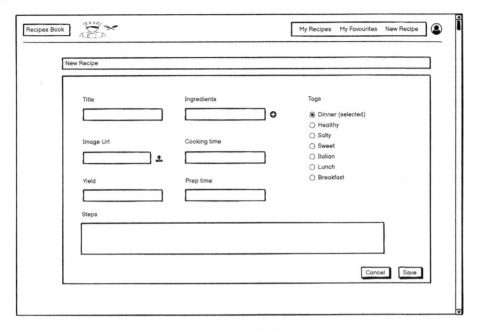

Figure 3.5 – The Modify Recipe view

View six – the recipe details interface

This contains all the details of the selected recipe.

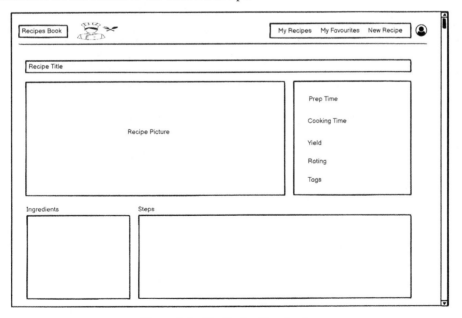

Figure 3.6 – The Recipe Details view

Our app's architecture

The frontend layer of the recipes book app will be implemented in Angular 12 and will communicate with a RESTful backend based on Node.js.

Note

The aspects related to the backend are not the subject of this book and will not be detailed. You can find the ready-to-use fake backend in the GitHub repository: `https://github.com/PacktPublishing/Reactive-Patterns-with-RxJS-7-in-Angular-applications`.

The frontend of the recipes book app is pluggable to any RESTful backend. Therefore, you can use pretty much any other technology for the backend. All communications will be performed through the HTTP Client module and will request REST controllers in the backend.

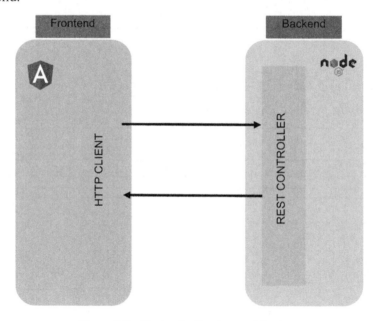

Figure 3.7 – The book of recipes architecture

The components overview

An Angular application is a tree structure consisting of all the components we create.

You will find below the components tree of our Recipes Book app, which is important for understanding the anatomy of the application:

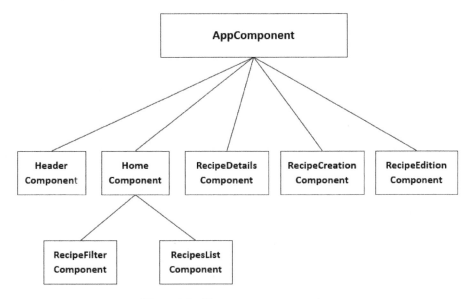

Figure 3.8 – The components overview

- **AppComponent**: The parent component of the app

- **Header Component**: The component representing the header of the app that contains the user space, the menu, and the logo

- **Home Component**: The component representing the landing page that contains **RecipeFilterComponent** and **RecipesListComponent**

- **RecipeFilterComponent**: The component representing the filter zone that contains the criteria fields, and the **Clear all** and **Show Results** buttons

- **RecipesListComponent**: The component containing the list of recipes

- **RecipesDetailsComponent**: The component containing the details of one recipe

- **RecipesCreationComponent**: The component containing a form to create a recipe with all the required fields

- **RecipesEditionComponent**: The component containing a form to edit a recipe with all the required fields

Summary

In this chapter, we explained the features of the recipes book application as well as the look and feel of the UI interfaces. We also shed light on the architecture and the components overview. Now that all those aspects are clear, let's explore the first reactive pattern together, which we will cover in the next chapter.

Part 2 –
A Trip into
Reactive Patterns

In this section, you will learn the most used reactive patterns in different real-world scenarios. Every reactive pattern will be endorsed by an example of implementation from the Angular application sample that we will build gradually.

This part comprises the following chapters:

4

Fetching Data as Streams

It is all about data! The way you manage your application's data has a huge impact on your UI performance and also the user experience. And, as far as I'm concerned, today, great user experience and performant UIs are no longer an option. In fact, they are key determinants of user satisfaction. Besides, managing data efficiently optimizes the code and enhances its quality, which consequently minimizes maintenance and improvement costs.

So, how can we manage our data efficiently? Well, this is what we will be answering in the following chapters. There are a few reactive patterns that come in handy in many use cases, and we will start by exploring the reactive pattern to fulfill a common and crucial use case, which is displaying values received from a REST endpoint for users to read and interact with.

We will start by explaining the requirement that we're going to implement in the RecipesBook application. Then, we will introduce the classic pattern to retrieve data, followed by the different approaches that you can use to manage unsubscriptions and all the important technical concepts surrounding them. Following this, we will explain the reactive pattern to fetch data. Finally, we will highlight the advantages of the reactive pattern over the classic one. Ready? Let's get started.

In this chapter, we're going to cover the following main topics:

- Defining the requirement
- Exploring the classic pattern for fetching data
- Exploring the reactive pattern for fetching data
- Highlighting the advantages of the reactive pattern.

Technical requirements

This chapter assumes that you have a basic understanding of HTTP Client.

We'll be using a mocked REST API using JSON Server, which allows you to spin up a REST API server with a fully working API. We'll not be learning how to use JSON Server, but if you are interested in learning more, you can find more information at `https://github.com/typicode/json-server`.

You can access the project source code for this chapter from the GitHub repository at `https://github.com/PacktPublishing/Reactive-Patterns-with-RxJS-for-Angular/tree/main/Chapter04`.

The project is composed of two folders:

- `recipes-book-api`: This contains the mocked server.
- `recipes-book-front`: This contains the frontend application that was built with Angular 12 and RxJS7 to help us build beautiful UI components quickly. Please refer to the previous chapter's Technical requirements.

The project complies with the standard Angular style guide, which can be found at `https://angular.io/guide/styleguide`.

You need to start the server by running the following command in the `recipes-book-api` folder:

```
npm run server:start
```

The server will be running at `http://localhost:3001`.

Then, you start the frontend by running the following command in the `recipes-book-front` folder:

```
ng serve --proxy-config proxy.config.json
```

You can read more about the `--proxy-config` parameter at `https://angular.io/guide/build#proxying-to-a-backend-server`

Defining the requirement

First, let's define the requirement we are going to fulfill in a reactive way. To define the requirement properly, we should answer this question: what do we want to do? Or, in other words, how should the application behave? Well, we want to display a list of recipes on the home page.

The component responsible for displaying the list of recipes is `RecipesListComponent`. So, we will display this component on the home page. We are going to progressively build the user story detailed in *View one – the landing page* section of *Chapter 3, A Walkthrough of the Application*.

Of course, we need to retrieve the list of recipes beforehand in order to display it to the user, right? So, the list of recipes represents the first **Data** that we need to request. This is available on a remote RESTful server. We are going to use a `GET` request and call the `/api/recipes` REST endpoint implemented in our `recipes-book-api` backend, which we started in the *Technical requirements* section.

In the following sections, we will explore the classic and recommended patterns used to fetch data.

Exploring the classic pattern for fetching data

Let's start by exploring the classic pattern for collecting our data. In our scenario, the requested data is the list of recipes.

Defining the structure of your data

First and foremost, we need to define the structure of our data so that we can strongly type it.

We can use the Angular CLI to generate the **Recipe** model underneath the `src/app/core/model` folder:

```
$ ng g i Recipe
```

For conventional purposes, we will change the name of the generated file from `recipe.ts` to `recipe.model.ts`. Then, we will populate the interface with the specific properties of `Recipe`, as follows:

```
export interface Recipe {

    id: number;
    title: string;
    ingredients: string;
    tags?: string;
    imageUrl: string;
    cookingTime?: number;
    prepTime?: number;
    yield: number;
    steps?: string;
    rating:number;
}
```

One by one, we put the properties of the recipe we are going to use followed by the type. The description of each property is detailed in *View two – the new recipe interface* section of *Chapter 3, A Walkthrough of the Application*.

For optional properties, we placed a question mark (?) just before the property's type annotation when declaring the interface.

Creating an Angular service

The next step is to create an Angular service named `RecipesService` that will be responsible for managing all the operations around the recipes. This service will encapsulate the **Create, Read, Update, and Delete (CRUD)** operations and make them available to the various UI components. In this chapter, we will only implement the read operation.

And why do we do this? Well, we do it to increase modularity in the first place and to ensure the reusability of the service over the other components.

We used the Angular CLI to generate the service underneath the `core/services` folder:

```
$  ng g s Recipes
```

Retrieving the data through a method

We will inject the `HttpClient` service and define a method to retrieve the data. The service will look like this:

```
import { Injectable } from '@angular/core';
import { HttpClient } from '@angular/common/http';
import { Observable } from 'rxjs';
import { Recipe } from '../model/recipe.model';
import { environment } from 'src/environments/environment';
const BASE_PATH = environment.basePath


@Injectable({
  providedIn: 'root'
})


export class RecipesService {


constructor(private http: HttpClient) { }


getRecipes(): Observable<Recipe[]> {
    return this.http.get<Recipe[]>(`${BASE_PATH}/recipes`);
  }
}
```

Let's break down what is going on at the level of this service. Well, it's nothing fancy!

We have a `getRecipes()` method that gets the list of recipes over HTTP and returns a strongly typed HTTP response: `Observable<Recipe[]>`. This `Observable` notifier represents the data stream that will be created when you issue the HTTP GET request. As a best practice, we externalized `BASE_PATH` in the `environment.ts` file because, in many cases, it depends on the environment.

Injecting and subscribing to the service in your component

Next, we will inject the service in the `RecipesListComponent` component, which is responsible for displaying the list of recipes, and call the `getRecipes()` method in `ngOnInit()` (when the component has been initialized). We are making a read operation against the API server.

In order to get the data emitted, we need to subscribe to the returned `Observable` notifier from the `getRecipes()` method. Then, we bind the data to a local property created in our component; in our case, this is the `recipes` array.

The component's code will look like this:

```
import { Component, OnInit } from '@angular/core';
import { Observable } from 'rxjs';
import { Recipe } from '../core/model/recipe';
import { RecipesService } from '../core/services/recipes.
service';

@Component({
  selector: 'app-recipes-list',
  templateUrl: './recipes-list.component.html',
  styleUrls: ['./recipes-list.component.css']
})
export class RecipesListComponent implements OnInit {

  recipes!: Recipe[];
  constructor(private service: RecipesService) { }

  ngOnInit(): void {
    this.service.getRecipes().subscribe(result => {
      this.recipes = result;
    });
  }

}
```

Now that we retrieved the data and stored it in a local property, let's see in the next section how we will display it in the UI.

Displaying the data in the template

Finally, we can use the `recipes` property (which is available in the component) in our HTML template to display the list of recipes in our UI. In our case, we are using the `DataView` PrimeNG component to display the list of recipes as cards in a grid layout. Further details can be found at `https://primefaces.org/primeng/showcase/#/dataview`.

Of course, our goal is not to focus on the template code, but the manipulation of the data inside it. As you can see, in the following example, we passed the `recipes` array to the `value` input of the data view component. You can also use structural directives to handle this with pure HTML if you don't want to include a third-party dependency:

```
<div class="card">
    <p-dataView #dv [value]="recipes" [paginator]="true"
     [rows]="9"      filterBy="name" layout="grid">
    /** Extra code here **/
    </p-dataView>
</div>
```

This is the basic pattern for collecting data, which we discovered back when we started to learn about Angular. So, you might have seen this before.

Just one thing left! You should handle the unsubscription of the observable, as this code manages subscriptions manually. Otherwise, the `Observable` notifier will not complete after the component has been destroyed, and the memory's reference will not be released, which will cause memory leaks.

Therefore, you should always be careful of this when manually subscribing to observables inside Angular components.

Managing unsubscriptions

There are two commonly used ways to manage unsubscriptions: the imperative pattern and the declarative and reactive patterns. Let's look at both of these patterns in detail.

Imperative unsubscription management

The imperative unsubscription means that we manually call the `unsubscribe()` method on the subscription object that we manage ourselves. The following code snippet illustrates this. We simply store the subscription inside a variable called `subscription` and unsubscribe from the `ngOnDestroy()` life cycle hook:

```
export class RecipesListComponent implements OnInit, OnDestroy
{

  recipes!: Recipe[];
  subscription: Subscription;
  constructor(private service: RecipesService) { }
```

```
ngOnInit(): void {
    this.subscription=this.service.getRecipes()
    .subscribe(result => {
        this.recipes = result;
    });
}

ngOnDestroy(): void {
    this.subscription.unsubscribe();
}
```

Well, this works fine, but it is not a recommended pattern. There are better ways of using the power of RxJS.

Declarative unsubscription management

The second way is far more declarative and cleaner; it uses the RxJS **takeUntil** operator. Before we dive into this pattern, let's gain an understanding of the role of **takeUntil**, and there is no better way to understand it than with a marble diagram.

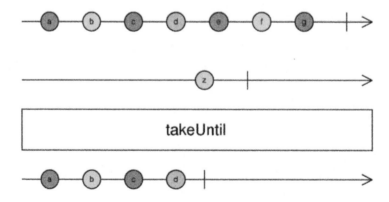

Figure 4.1 – The takeUntil marble diagram

The `takeUntil()` operator takes values from the source observable (the first timeline) until the `Observable` notifier, which is given as input (the second timeline), emits a value. In the previous marble diagram, the source observable emitted the values of **a**, **b**, **c**, and **d**. So, `takeUntil()` will emit them, respectively. After that, the `Observable` notifier emits **z**. So, `takeUntil()` will stop emitting values and will complete.

The takeUntil operator will help us keep the subscription alive for a period that we define. We want it to be alive until the component has been destroyed, so we will create an RxJS subject that will emit a value when the component has been destroyed. Then, we will pass this subject to takeUntil as input:

```
recipes!: Recipe[];
destroy$ = new Subject<void>();
constructor(private service: RecipesService) { }


ngOnInit(): void {
  this.service.getRecipes().pipe(
  takeUntil(this.destroy$)).
  subscribe(result => {
    this.recipes = result;
  });
}

ngOnDestroy(): void {
  this.destroy$.next();
  this.destroy$.complete();


}
```

> **Note**
>
> The $ sign is an informal convention that is used to indicate that the variable is an Observable notifier. You can read more about the trailing $ sign on the Angular website at https://angular.io/guide/rx-library#naming-conventionsfor-observables.

And that's it! We're done.

The first thing you might notice here is that it's less code than the first approach. Furthermore, when we call unsubscribe() on a returned subscription object (the first way), there's no way we can be notified that the unsubscription happened. However, using takeUntil(), in this case, you will be notified of the observable completion through the completion handler.

Additionally, you can use other operators that manage the unsubscription for you in a more reactive way. For example, take a look at the following:

- `take(X)`: This emits *x* values and then completes. However, bear in mind that if your network is slow and the *xth* emission didn't happen, then you have to unsubscribe.

- `first()`: This emits the first value and then completes.

- `last()`: This emits the last value and then completes.

This was the classic pattern that we learned at the beginning, and it is a relatively valid way. To sum up, the following diagram describes all the steps that we walked through:

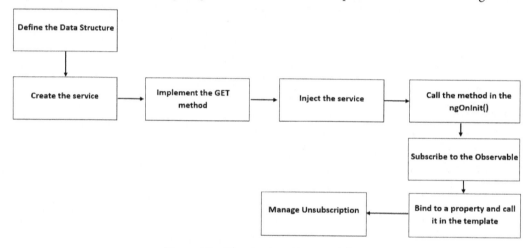

Figure 4.2 – The classic pattern workflow

However, there is another pattern that we can use, which is much more **declarative** and **reactive** and has many advantages. Let's discover it next!

Exploring the reactive pattern for fetching data

The idea behind this reactive pattern is to keep and use the observable as a stream throughout the application. Don't worry; this will become more apparent to you later in this section.

Retrieving data as streams

So, instead of defining a method to retrieve our data, we will declare a variable inside our service:

```
import { Injectable } from '@angular/core';
import { HttpClient } from '@angular/common/http';
import { Observable } from 'rxjs';
import { Recipe } from '../model/recipe';
import { environment } from 'src/environments/environment';
const BASE_PATH = environment.basePath


@Injectable({
  providedIn: 'root'
})
export class RecipesService {

  recipes$ = this.http.get<Recipe[]>(
    `${BASE_PATH}/recipes`);
  constructor(private http: HttpClient) { }
}
```

Here, we are declaring the `recipes$` variable as the result of HTTP GET, which is either an observable or the data stream.

Defining the stream in your component

Now, in `RecipesListComponent`, we are going to do the same thing we did in the classic pattern, that is, declaring a variable holding the stream returned from our service. This time, the variable is an observable:

```
import { Component, OnDestroy, OnInit } from '@angular/core';
import { RecipesService } from '../core/services/recipes.
service';

@Component({
  selector: 'app-recipes-list',
  templateUrl: './recipes-list.component.html',
```

```
    styleUrls: ['./recipes-list.component.css']
})
export class RecipesListComponent implements OnInit {

  recipes$= this.service.recipes$;

    constructor(private service: RecipesService) { }
}
```

But wait! We need to subscribe in order to get the emitted data, right? That's absolutely right.

Using the async pipe in your template

We will not subscribe manually; instead, we will use the **async pipe**.

The async pipe makes rendering values emitted from the observable easier. First of all, it automatically subscribes to the input observable. Then, it returns the latest value emitted. And best of all, when the component has been destroyed, it automatically unsubscribes to avoid any potential memory leaks.

This means there is no need to clean up any subscriptions when the component has been destroyed. And that's amazing. Whenever a new value is emitted, it marks the component to be checked for changes.

So, in the template, we bind to an observable using the async pipe. Here, as recipes describes the array variable that the values are emitted into. We can use it in the template as follows:

```
<div *ngIf="recipes$ |async as recipes" class="card">
    <p-dataView #dv [value]="recipes" [paginator]="true"
    [rows]="9"      filterBy="name" layout="grid">
    /** Extra code here **/
    </p-dataView>
</div>
```

By doing this, we don't need the ngOnInit life cycle hook. We will not subscribe to the Observable notifier in ngOnInit() and unsubscribe from ngOnDestroy(), as we did in the classic pattern. We simply set a local property in our component, and we are good to go.

So, you don't need to handle the subscription and unsubscription on your own.

The total code of the HTML template is available in the GitHub repository.

To sum up, the following diagram describes all the steps we walked through:

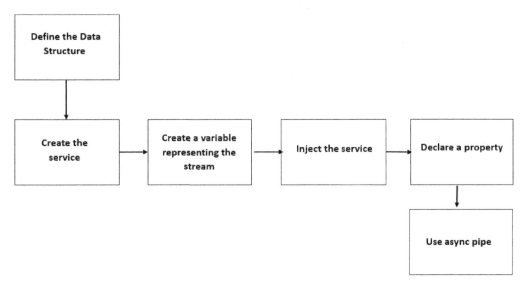

Figure 4.3 – The reactive pattern workflow

Now that we have explained the reactive pattern in action, in the next section, let's discover its advantages.

Highlighting the advantages of the reactive pattern

I think you might have guessed the first advantage: we don't have to manually manage subscriptions and unsubscriptions, and what a relief! But there are a lot of other advantages; it is not only about the async pipe. Let's look at the other advantages in more detail.

Using the declarative approach

Let's shed light on the fact that we don't explicitly use the subscribe() method. What's wrong with subscribe()? Well, subscribing to a stream inside our component means we are allowing imperative code to leak into our functional and reactive code. Using the RxJS observables does not make your code reactive and declarative systematically. But what does declarative mean exactly?

Well, first, we will nail down some key terms. Then, let's iterate from there:

- **Declarative** refers to the use of declared functions to perform actions. You rely upon pure functions that can define an event flow. With RxJS, you can see this in the form of observables and operators.

- A **pure function** is a function that will always return identical outputs for identical inputs, no matter how many times it is called. In other words, the function will always predictably produce the same output.

So, why should you care? Well, you should care because the declarative approach using RxJS operators and observables has many advantages, namely, the following:

- It makes your code cleaner and more readable.

- It makes your code easier to test because it is predictable.

- It makes you able to cache the stream output given a certain input, and this will enhance performance. We will explore this in more detail in *Chapter 8, Multicasting Essentials, Chapter 9, Caching Streams*, and *Chapter 10, Sharing Data between Components*.

- It enables you to leverage RxJS operators and transform and combine streams coming from different services or even within the same service. This is what we will see in *Chapter 7, Transforming Streams*.

- It helps you react easily to user interactions in order to execute an action.

So, more declarative means more reactive. However, be careful. This doesn't mean you can't ever call the `subscribe()` method. It is unavoidable in some situations to trigger the `Observable` notifier. But try to ask yourself, do I really need to subscribe here? Can I instead compose multiple streams together, or use RxJS operators, to achieve what I need without subscribing? Aside from cases where it is unavoidable, never use `subscribe()`.

Now, let's move to the performance advantages.

Using the change detection strategy of OnPush

The other really cool thing is that we can use the `changeDetection` strategy, `OnPush`.

Change detection is one of the powerful features of Angular. It is about detecting when the component's data changes and then automatically re-rendering the view or updating the DOM to reflect that change. The default strategy of "check always" means that, whenever any data is mutated or changed, Angular will run the change detector to update the DOM. So, it is automatic until explicitly deactivated.

In the `OnPush` strategy, Angular will only run the change detector when the following occurs:

- **Condition 1**: A component's `@Input` property reference changes (bear in mind that when the input property object is mutated directly then the reference of the object will not change and consequently the change detector will not run. In this case we should return a new reference of the property object to trigger the change detection).

- **Condition 2**: A component event handler is emitted or gets triggered.

- **Condition 3**: A bound observable via the async pipe emits a new value.

Therefore, using the `changeDetection OnPush` strategy minimizes any change detection cycles and will only check for changes to re-render our components in the preceding cases. This strategy applies to all child directives and cannot be overridden.

In our scenario, we only need the change detector to run if we get a new value; otherwise, we get useless updates. So, our scenario matches **Condition 3**. The good news is that we can use the change detection `onPush` strategy as follows:

```
import { ChangeDetectionStrategy, Component} from '@angular/
core';

@Component({
  selector: 'app-recipes-list',
  templateUrl: './recipes-list.component.html',
  styleUrls: ['./recipes-list.component.scss'],
  changeDetection: ChangeDetectionStrategy.OnPush
})
```

So, if we remember to use the async pipe as much as possible, we will see a couple of advantages:

- We will make it easier to switch from the default change detection strategy to `OnPush` later if we need to.

- We will run into fewer change detection cycles using `OnPush`.

Using the async pipe will help you to achieve a high-performing UI, and it will have a lot of impact if our view is doing multiple tasks.

And here's the output of our UI:

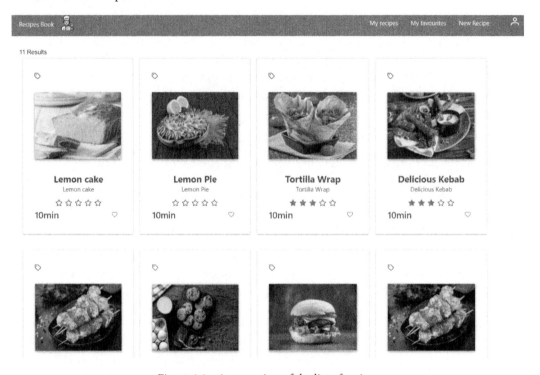

Figure 4.4 – An overview of the list of recipes

Wrapping up

In a nutshell, using the reactive pattern for fetching data will ensure the following:

- It improves the performance of your application.
- It improves the change detection strategy.
- It improves code clarity and readability.
- It makes the code more declarative and more reactive.
- It makes it easier to leverage RxJS operators.
- It makes it easier to react to user action.

Summary

In this chapter, we explored the classic and reactive patterns for fetching data. We learned the imperative way in which to manage unsubscriptions and the reactive pattern. We explained some useful RxJS operators and also shed light on the advantages of using the reactive pattern and we learned about all the technical aspects around.

Now that we have retrieved our data as RxJS streams, in the next chapters, let's start playing with those streams to react to user actions using RxJS streams and, consequently, build our RecipesApp application in a reactive way. In the next chapter, we will focus on the reactive patterns for error handling and the different strategies that are available.

5

Error Handling

Error handling is a crucial part of every application. Errors in programming happen all the time, and RxJS is no exception; implementing a process that only covers happy cases determines the failure of your application. I always say this to my students in every training session. In RxJS, there are a lot of error handling strategies that you need to learn in order to handle errors efficiently.

We will start by explaining the contract of the Observable in RxJS, which is crucial to understand what comes after. Then, we will learn the different error handling patterns and the operators provided by RxJS for that purpose. Next, we will shed light on the different error handling strategies and the use case of every strategy. Finally, we will practice one of the error handling strategies in our recipes app.

In this chapter, we're going to cover the following main topics:

- Understanding the anatomy of an Observable
- Exploring error handling patterns and strategies
- Error handling in action

Technical requirements

This chapter assumes that you have a basic understanding of RxJS. The source code of this chapter except the samples is available at `https://github.com/PacktPublishing/Reactive-Patterns-with-RxJS-for-Angular/tree/main/Chapter05`.

Please refer to the *Technical requirements* section in *Chapter 4, Fetching Data as Streams*.

Understanding the anatomy of an Observable

Understanding the Observable anatomy is crucial in order to learn error handling patterns. Do you remember this marble diagram, explained in *Chapter 1, The Power of the Reactive Paradigm*?

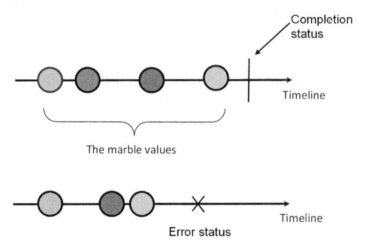

Figure 5.1 – The marble diagram elements

Let's examine the preceding diagram. If we look closer at the stream's life cycle, we can figure out that a stream has two final statuses:

- **Completion status**: When the stream has ended without errors and will not emit any further values. It is a SHUT DOWN.

- **Error status**: When the stream has ended with an error and will not emit any further values after the error is thrown. It is also a SHUT DOWN.

Only one of those two states can occur, not both, and every stream can error out once. This is the Observable contract. You may be wondering at this point, how we can recover from an error then?

This is what we will be learning in the following sections.

Exploring error handling patterns and strategies

The first classic pattern we will learn for handling errors is based on the `subscribe()` method. The `subscribe()` method takes as input the object Observer, which has three callbacks:

- **A success callback**: This is called every time the stream emits a value and receives as input the value emitted.

- **An error callback**: This is called when an error occurs and receives as input the error itself.

- **A completion callback**: This is called when the stream completes.

So, in order to handle the error, the first possibility is implementing the error callback. In the following code sample, `stream$` represents our Observable, and we implemented the following:

- A success callback that logs the received value in the console

- An error callback that logs the received error in the console

- A complete callback that logs the stream completion:

```
stream$.subscribe({
  next: (res) => console.log('Value Emitted', res),
  error: (err) => console.log('Error Occurred', err),
  complete: () => console.log('Stream Completed'),
});
```

Pretty simple, but wait! In the previous chapter, *Chapter 4*, *Fetching Data as Streams*, we saw that we need to avoid the explicit `subscribe()` to the streams and learned the reasons and limitations behind this. So, in most cases, we will not be using `subscribe()` explicitly – that's right! But I just wanted to show you the classic way to do this, which is not the recommended way. In fact, handling errors using the `subscribe()` method has a few limitations, namely that it is impossible to recover from the error or emit an alternative fallback.

Let's see some advanced error handling patterns and learn more operators that will help us in the error handling process.

Handling error operators

I think you may be familiar with the try-catch statement available in many programming languages, which consists of a `try` block followed by one or more `catch` clauses. In the `try` block, you place your risky statements, and inside `catch`, you handle the possible exceptions:

```
try {
    // risky statements
}
catch(error) {
    // handle exceptions
}
```

RxJS ships with the `catchError` operator, which provides us with something close to the try-catch statement.

The catchError operator

`catchError`, according to the RxJS official documentation, "*catches errors on the observable to be handled by returning a new observable or throwing an error.*"

The `catchError` operator subscribes to the source Observable that might error out and emits values to the observer until an error occurs. When that happens, the `catchError` operator executes a callback function, passing in the error. This callback function is responsible for handling errors **and always returns an Observable**.

If there are no errors, the output Observable returned by `catchError` works exactly the same way as the source Observable. You can use `catchError` multiple times in an Observable chain:

```
import { catchError} from 'rxjs/operators';

//stream$ is the source Observable that might error out
stream$.pipe(
    catchError(error => {
        //handle the error received
    })
    ).subscribe()
}
```

When it comes to handling errors, there are three strategies:

- A replace strategy
- A rethrow strategy
- A retry strategy

Let's break down these three strategies one by one.

A replace strategy

The error handling function returns an Observable, which is going to be a replacement Observable for the stream that just errored out. This replacement Observable is then going to be subscribed to, and its values are going to be used in place of the errored-out input Observable:

```
import { from, of } from 'rxjs';
import { catchError, map } from 'rxjs/operators';

const stream$ = from(['5', '10', '6', 'Hello', '2']);
stream$
  .pipe(
    map((value) => {
      if (isNaN(value as any)) {
        throw new Error('This is not a number');
      }
      return parseInt(value);
    }),
    catchError((error) => {
      console.log('Caught Error', error);
      return of();
    })
  )
  .subscribe({
    next: (res) => console.log('Value Emitted', res),
    error: (err) => console.log('Error Occurred', err),
    complete: () => console.log('Stream Completed'),
  });
```

```
//output
Value Emitted 5
Value Emitted 10
Value Emitted 6
Caught Error Error: This is not a number
Stream Completed
```

Let's break down what is happening at the level of this sample.

We have an Observable stream$ created from an array of string values, ['5', '10', '6', 'Hello', '2'], using the from creation operator.

> **Note**
>
> For more details about the from operator, please refer to this link from the official documentation: https://rxjs.dev/api/index/function/from#description.

We use two operators on stream$:

- The map operator: To transform the string values emitted to integers using the parseInt() method. If the value emitted is not a number, then the "This is not a number" error is thrown.

- The catchError operator: We pass to it the error handling function that will log the catched error and return an empty of() Observable.

Then, we subscribe to the stream$ and log a custom message in every callback.

What happens at execution time?

At execution time, stream$ will emit the string values of the array one by one, respectively '5', '10', and '6'. The map takes those values one by one as input and returns respectively the 5, 10, and 6 integers. catchError() takes the values emitted from the map operator and forwards them as output; the error handling function will not get called, as there is no error. Hence, the subscribers receive 5, 10, and 6.

catchError() comes into play when the 'Hello' value is emitted. The map operator will throw an error, and the error handling function in catchError() will get called consequently.

The error handling function in our case simply logs an error in the console and returns an empty Observable in this example. This empty Observable will be the replacement Observable.

`catchError()` will subscribe under the hood to the returned Observable. The `of()` Observable will emit a value and complete. The empty value is emitted and then `stream$` is completed, so the second value will not get emitted.

As you may have noticed, the error callback in the `subscribe()` method will not get called because we handled it. I added it on purpose to understand the behavior of error handling with `catchError`.

Therefore, when an error occurs, the current stream that errored out will get replaced by the stream returned from the `catchError()`; the values of the replaced Observable will then get emitted instead of the original stream values. This is what we call fallback values.

A rethrow strategy

A rethrow strategy consists in rethrowing the error or, in other words, propagating the error to the subscribers of the output Observable of `catchError`. This propagation mechanism allows you to rethrow the error caught by `catchError` and not only handle it locally. Let's look at this example, which is the same as the replace strategy one. The only difference is in the handling error function:

```
import { from, throwError } from 'rxjs';
import { catchError, map } from 'rxjs/operators';


const stream$ = from(['5', '10', '6', 'Hello', '2']);
stream$
  .pipe(
    map((value) => {
      if (isNaN(value as any)) {
        throw new Error('This is not a number');
      }
      return parseInt(value);
    }),
    catchError((error) => {
      console.log('Caught Error', error);
      return throwError(() => error);
    })
  )
```

```
  .subscribe({
    next: (res) => console.log('Value Emitted', res),
    error: (err) => console.log('Error Occurred', err),
    complete: () => console.log('Stream Completed'),
  });


//output
Value Emitted 5
Value Emitted 10
Value Emitted 6
Caught Error Error: This is not a number
Error Occurred Error: This is not a number
```

In the handle error function, we return an Observable that is created using the throwError operator. throwError creates an Observable that never emits any value. Instead, it errors out immediately using the same error caught by catchError.

In other words, the output Observable of catchError will also error out with the exact same error thrown by the source Observable. The error can now be further handled by the rest of the Observable chain, if needed. As you may have noticed, the same error was logged both in the catchError block and in the subscriber error handler function, as expected.

Please note that in the previous examples, we simply log the error in the console for demonstration purposes. But in a real-world scenario, you can do much more, such as showing messages to the users.

A retrying strategy

You can also retry the observable using the retry operator to give another chance to the stream. The retry operator retries an Observable a specific number of times. It is useful for retrying HTTP requests, for example:

```
import { catchError, map, retry } from 'rxjs/operators';
import { from, throwError } from 'rxjs';

const stream$ = from(['5', '10', '6', 'Hello', '2']);
stream$
  .pipe(
```

```
    map((value) => {
      if (isNaN(value as any)) {
        throw new Error('This is not a number');
      }
      return parseInt(value);
    }),
    retry(2),
    catchError((error) => {
      console.log('Caught Error', error);
      return throwError(() => error);
    })
  )
  .subscribe({
    next: (res) => console.log('Value Emitted', res),
    error: (err) => console.log('Error Occurred', err),
    complete: () => console.log('Stream Completed'),
  });


//output
Value Emitted 5
10
6
5
10
6
5
10
6

Caught Error Error: This is not a number
Error Occurred Error: This is not a number
```

As you may have noticed, the values of the source stream were emitted two times because we gave the observable a chance two times before throwing the error. In fact, we called the retry operator with 2 as input.

In this case, we are retrying immediately. But what if we want to retry in only specific cases or wait for a delay before retrying? Here comes the `retryWhen` operator into play!

The retryWhen operator

To understand the `retryWhen` operator, there's nothing better than a marble diagram:

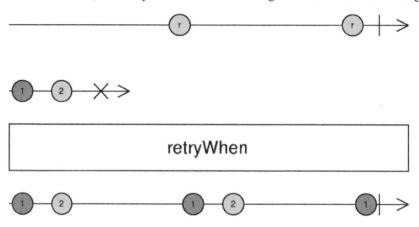

Figure 5.2 – The retryWhen operator

Now, let's explain what is going on in this marble diagram:

- The Observable in the first line is **the notifier observable** that is going to determine when the retry should occur.

- The Observable in the second line is **the source observable** that will error out after emitting **1** and **2**.

The source Observable emits **1** and **2** (after getting subscribed to obviously). The `retryWhen` forwards those values as output. Then, the source Observable errors out and completes.

Nothing will happen until the notifier Observable emits **r**. At that moment, the source Observable will get retried, and as you see, **1** and **2** get emitted again. In fact, `retryWhen` will subscribe to the source Observable because it is already completed, so even if it is completed, it can be retried.

The notifier Observable is then going to emit another **r** value, and the same thing occurs.

`retryWhen` starts to emit the first **1** value, but soon after, the notifier Observable completes; that's why the **2** value will not get emitted.

As you may have guessed, `retryWhen` retries the source Observable each time the notifier emits a value! This means that you can use this notifier Observable to emit values at the moment you want your source Observable to get retried and complete it at the moment you want your retry attempts to stop.

Now, let's have a look at the signature of the `retryWhen` operator:

```
export declare function retryWhen<T>(notifier:
(errors: Observable<any>) => Observable<any>):
MonoTypeOperatorFunction<T>;
```

The `notifier` parameter represents the callback that returns the notifier Observable and gets the error Observable as the argument. The error Observable will emit every time the source Observable errors out. `retryWhen` subscribes to the notifier Observable and behaves as described previously.

Here's the same example given in the replace and rethrow strategies with `retryWhen`:

```
import { from} from 'rxjs';
import { map, retryWhen, tap } from 'rxjs/operators';


const stream$ = from(['5', '10', '6', 'Hello', '2']);
stream$
  .pipe(
    map((value) => {
      if (isNaN(value as any)) {
        throw new Error('This is not a number');
      }
      return parseInt(value);
    }),
    retryWhen((errors) => {
      return errors.pipe(
        tap(() => console.log('Retrying the source
                        Observable...'))
      );
    })
  )
  .subscribe({
    next: (res) => console.log('Value Emitted', res),
    error: (err) => console.log('Error Occurred', err),
```

```
    complete: () => console.log('Stream Completed'),
  });




//Code runs infinitely
```

In this case, the errors are caught by the `retryWhen` operator. Our notifier callback takes simply the error Observable as input and returns it. We used the pipe to call the tap operator for logging purposes (to log the Retrying message in the console).

> **Note**
>
> For more details about the tap operator, please refer to this link from the official documentation: `https://rxjs.dev/api/operators/tap`.

If you execute that code, you will find out that it runs infinitely. Why? Because the source will always error out, and `retryWhen` will consequently subscribe infinitely to the source Observable.

If the source always errors out, it is not correct to retry immediately. However, the error will not always occur – for example, in the case of HTTP requests. Sometimes, the HTTP request fails because the server is down, or there is another reason that may disappear, and the request might go through in the next attempts without any problem.

In that case, you can use the immediate retry or even a delayed retry, which is retrying after a certain delay where we can wait, for example, for 5 seconds after the error occurs before retrying.

The delayWhen operator

To understand the `delayWhen` operator, there's nothing better than a marble diagram:

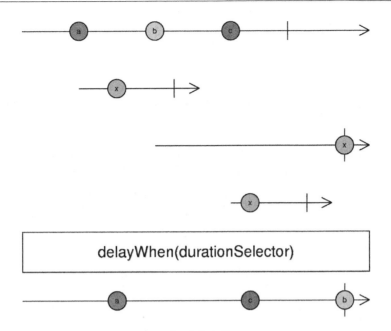

Figure 5.3 – The delayWhen operator

The first Observable is the source Observable. Every value emitted by the source Observable will be delayed before being emitted to the output Observable. The delay is completely flexible through the durationSelector function.

Each of the **a**, **b**, and **c** values has its own duration selector Observable, which will emit one value and then complete. When the selector emits a value, the corresponding **a**, **b**, or **c** input value is going to show up in the output of delayWhen.

As you can see, the selector of **b** emitted the last one; that's why the **b** value was emitted last.

Another function, the timer function, can be useful in the delayed retry strategy:

```
export declare function timer(dueTime?: number | Date,
periodOrScheduler?: number | SchedulerLike, scheduler?:
SchedulerLike): Observable<number>;
```

This timer function returns an Observable and takes two arguments:

- due: A time period or exact date, before which no values will be emitted

- scheduler: A periodic interval, in case we want to emit new values periodically

An example is `timer(5000,1000)`. The first value of the returned Observable will get emitted after 5 seconds, and a new value is emitted each second. The second argument is optional, which means that `timer(5000)` will emit a value after 5 seconds and then complete.

Now, it is time to combine those operators to see how we can retry a failing HTTP request 5 seconds after each error:

```typescript
import { Injectable } from '@angular/core';
import { HttpClient } from '@angular/common/http';
import { Recipe } from '../model/recipe.model';
import { catchError, delayWhen, of, retryWhen, tap, timer }
from 'rxjs';
@Injectable({
  providedIn: 'root'
})

export class RecipesService {

recipes$ = this.http.get<Recipe[]>('http://localhost:3001/
recipes').pipe(
    retryWhen(errors => {
      return errors
        .pipe(
          delayWhen(() => timer(5000)),
          tap(() => console.log('Retrying the HTTP
                                 request...'))
        );
    }),
  );
  constructor(private http: HttpClient) { }
}
```

> **Note**
>
> You will not find the preceding code in the GitHub repository, as it is just a sample. However, you can copy and paste it into the `RecipesService` class in order to test the delayed retry.

Our source Observable, in this case, is the result of an HTTP `get` request. Each time the request fails, the `delayWhen` operator creates a duration selector Observable through the `timer` function. This duration selector Observable is going to emit the 0 value after 5 seconds and then complete. Therefore, the notifier Observable of `retryWhen` will emit a value, and at that moment, the source Observable will get retried, after 5 seconds to be exact.

When you open the console, you will see this output:

Figure 5.4 – The failing HTTP request

That's it. This is how we achieved a delayed retry.

Now that we have learned the different strategies and operators to handle errors, let's practice in our Recipes app in the next section.

Error handling in action

The first thing we are going to do is stop our mock service. Yes, you heard it right – stop it. This way, the call to the `getRecipes` service will fail because the server is down.

Now, if you refresh the front app, you will see that nothing is displayed. Our list of recipes is not displayed. Why do we get this behavior? Because we did not handle the errors. The error was thrown, the stream completed, and nothing happened afterward. We have a white screen where nothing is displayed. Open the console, and you will see the failed request:

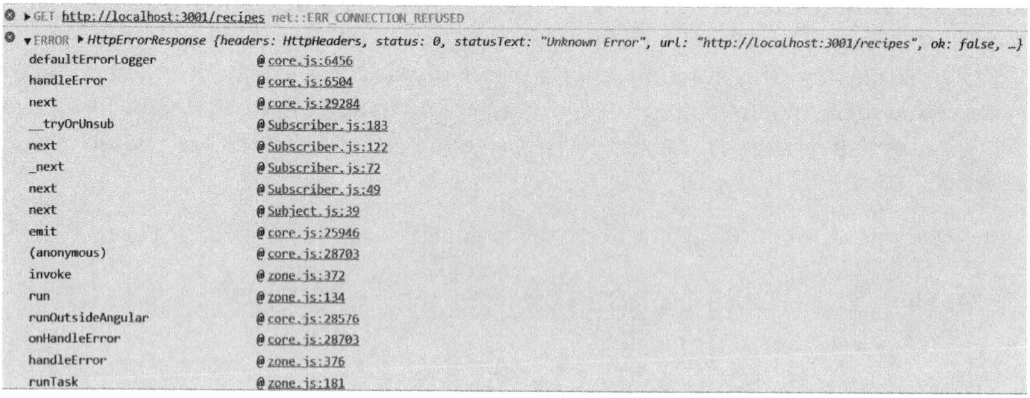

Figure 5.5 – The console showing the failed request

You should be very careful about all the HTTP requests you raise in particular and all the processes in your front application in general. It is amazing to work with streams… when they are safe. So, how can we fix this? Just remember the strategies I have just told you. What strategy should we choose?

By the way, the last example in the previous section is picked from the Recipe app. We retried getting the recipes after 5 seconds from each failure. Is this the right strategy? In our case, if we choose the rethrow or retry strategy, we will block the display of the recipes list. We will get a blank page. The user will wait for the request to get executed successfully in order to see the UI. This is not correct. It is correct when you have processes in the background or processes that are not related to the UI display. But if you raise requests in order to get results and display data in your UI components, then you should provide a replacement for that data to continue rendering the page.

That's why our case falls under the replacement strategy. In fact, we want to get the list of recipes from the service, but if the service fails for whatever reason, I don't want my application to be frozen; I want to see a collection of zero elements (no elements), an empty table, or a list, and that is all. So, what we are going to do is use catchError and return an empty Observable, which is our fallback value.

Our service will look like this:

```
import { Injectable } from '@angular/core';
import { HttpClient } from '@angular/common/http';
import { Recipe } from '../model/recipe.model';
import { environment } from 'src/environments/environment';
import { catchError, of } from 'rxjs';
const BASE_PATH = environment.basePath

@Injectable({
  providedIn: 'root'
})

export class RecipesService {

  recipes$ = this.http.get<Recipe[]>(
    '${BASE_PATH}/recipes').pipe(
    catchError(error => of([])));

  constructor(private http: HttpClient) { }
}
```

This way, your application will keep on working, and if you open the app, you will see an empty list.

Summary

In this chapter, we explored some of the most commonly used RxJS error handling strategies available. We learned about the Observable contract. We explained some useful RxJS operators to handle errors, namely catchError(), delayWhen(), retry(), and retryWhen(). We also shed light on the different strategies for error handling and when to choose each strategy. Finally, we handled the error in our Recipes app for the first implemented feature.

Now that we know how to handle errors in RxJS, let's move on to the next reactive pattern – combining streams.

6
Combining Streams

Now that we have learned about how to use the reactive pattern to fetch data as streams and have covered the error handling patterns, let's start playing with streams. One of the most powerful utilities provided by RxJS that I have found extremely useful is the combination of streams, and this is the heart of this chapter.

This chapter revolves around a common use case, filtering data, that we will resolve by combining streams. We will start by explaining the requirement, and then we will explore the imperative, classic pattern that can be used to implement this requirement followed by a look at the declarative, reactive pattern for it.

In this chapter, we're going to cover the following main topics:

- Defining the requirement
- Exploring the imperative pattern for filtering data
- Exploring the declarative pattern for filtering data

Technical requirements

This chapter assumes that you have a basic understanding of RxJS.

The source code of this chapter except the samples is available at `https://github.com/PacktPublishing/Reactive-Patterns-with-RxJS-for-Angular/tree/main/Chapter06`.

Defining the requirement

We want to filter the displayed recipes according to some criteria to refine the results. The following figure shows the implementation of the mockup described in the *View one – the landing page* section of *Chapter 3, A Walkthrough of the Application*:

Figure 6.1 – The filtering requirement

From a user's perspective, the user will fill out some criteria in the **Filters** area and click on the **See results** button to see the results that match the filled criteria. The user can filter by keywords in the recipe title, recipe category, ingredients, tags, preparation, and cooking time. A filtering functionality is a must in the majority of applications that display data collections.

When it comes to filtering, there are a lot of strategies you can adopt, and your choice of them depends highly on the size of your data. If you have a small amount of data that you fetch entirely on the client side, then it is unnecessary to perform server-side filtering; it is faster to perform client-side filtering, which would not harm your application's performance. However, if you have a large amount of data, then you should be lazy loading your data through pagination, infinite scroll, or virtual scroll, in order to enhance the performance and the user experience as well. Therefore, doing server-side filtering in this case is unavoidable, since you don't have all the data on the client side.

In our case, it is a sample app and we have only 11 recipes in total. So, we're going to use client-side filtering, but the reactive pattern we're going to discuss does not need a specific type of filtering: it can be used with both client- and server-side filtering.

Exploring the imperative pattern for filtering data

Let's look at the classic, or imperative, way of filtering data, which is not the recommended way.

The first thing that comes to mind is defining an `OnClick` callback to execute when the **See results** button is clicked and calling a method that will replace the displayed recipes with those that match the filled criteria. Then the UI will be updated automatically thanks to the Angular change detection mechanism.

A look at the filter component

We generated a new component, `RecipesFilterComponent`, under `src/app/recipes-filter`. It is responsible for displaying the different filters to refine the initial results. The HTML template of the filter component looks like this:

```
<div class="rp-filters">
    <form [formGroup]="recipeForm">
        <fieldset class="rp-filters-group">
            <legend>Filters</legend>
            <div class="rp-filter-button">
                <p-button (onClick)="clearFilter()"
                label="Clear all"></p-button>
            </div>
            <label for="title">Keyword:</label>
            <input type="text" id="title"
             formControlName="title">
            <label for="category">Category:</label>
            <input type="text" id="category"
             formControlName="category">
            <label for="ingredient">Ingredient:</label>
            <input type="text" id="ingredient"
             formControlName="ingredient">
```

```
            <label for="text">Tags:</label>
            <input type="text" id="tags"
             formControlName="tags">
            <label for="text">Preparation Time:</label>
            <input type="text" id="prepTime"
             formControlName="prepTime">
            <label for="text">Cooking Time:</label>
            <input type="text" id="cookingTime"
             formControlName="cookingTime">
            <div class="rp-filter-button">
                <p-button class="rp-filter-button"
                (onClick)="filterResults()" label="See
                results"></p-button>
            </div>
        </fieldset>
    </form>
</div>
```

We used Angular Reactive forms to display the search criteria.

> **Note**
>
> For more details about Reactive forms, please refer to `https://angular.io/guide/reactive-forms`.

We have two buttons, the **Clear all** button to clear the filters and the **See results** button to refine the displayed items by calling the `filterResults()` method on click.

A look at the recipes list component

There is a small change that we should consider in the `RecipesListComponent` template. We should bind the `[value]` input of the `p-dataView` component to a new property, the `filtredRecipes` property that holds the filtered results. `filtredRecipes` initially holds all the requested recipes from the server. This is what the template looks like:

```
<div class="card">
    <p-dataView #dv [value]="filtredRecipes"
    [paginator]="true" [rows]="9"        filterBy="name"
```

```
        layout="grid">
        /** Extra code here **/
        </p-dataView>
</div>
```

The focus is not the HTML template, of course, but the process of filtering. However, it is important to point it out to provide a complete workflow.

Now let's look at the logic of the classic pattern in `RecipesListComponent`:

```
export class RecipesListComponent implements OnInit, OnDestroy
{

  filtredRecipes: Recipe[] = [];
  recipes: Recipe[] = [];
  private destroy$: Subject<boolean> = new
   Subject<boolean>();

  constructor(private service: RecipesService, private fb:
   FormBuilder) {
  }

  ngOnInit(): void {
     this.service.recipes$.pipe(takeUntil(this.destroy$))
       .subscribe((recipes) => {
         this.recipes = recipes;
         this.filtredRecipes = recipes;
      });
  }


  ngOnDestroy(): void {
     this.destroy$.next(true);
     this.destroy$.unsubscribe();
  }


  filterResults() {
```

```
this.filtredRecipes = this.recipes.filter(recipe =>
  recipe.title?.indexOf(this.recipeForm.value.title) !=
  -1)
}
```

Let's break down what is happening here. We declared four variables:

- `filtredRecipes`: The array that contains the filtered recipes. It is the property binded in the HTML template to the `[value]` input of the `p-dataview` component.

- `recipes`: The initial array of recipes.

- `destroy$`: A subject to clean up the subscription.

In the `ngOninit()` method, we call the recipes (`recipes$`) that represent our Observable of recipes. Then, we subscribe to it and initialize the recipes and `filteredRecipes` arrays with the emitted array from `recipes$`.

As we don't use the async pipe in this example, we should clean up the subscription manually using the `takeUntil()` pattern as explained in the *Exploring the classic pattern for fetching data* section of *Chapter 4, Fetching Data as Streams*.

The `filterResults()` method called when clicking on the **See results** button filters the current recipes list and returns the recipes that match the filter. In this sample, we considered only the title when filtering the criteria. The criteria are retrieved from the reactive form value through `this.recipeForm.value.title;` it contains the value the user filled out in the title input.

If you perform server-side filtering, `filterResults()` will look like this:

```
filterResults() {
  this.filtredRecipes =
    this.http.get<Recipe[]>(`${BASE_PATH}/recipes`,
    {params:{criteria:this.recipeForm.value}});

}
```

And that's it! It works fine, and I would say this is probably how most people would approach implementing something like this in an Angular application. It's kind of the obvious way to do it. At the same time, this is the imperative way to do it. You may have noticed that we are no longer able to take advantage of `recipes$` as a stream in the template as explained in *Chapter 4, Fetching Data as Streams*.

Plus, what if your recipes service emits new recipes? This will overwrite the active filter until the user clicks on **See results** again to update the list with the current filter. This can be handled imperatively, of course, but it is a shame to use observables and not take advantage of the power of the reactivity. And I really want to always highlight the classic way and the reactive way right after to enable a smooth transition from imperative to declarative.

So, without further ado, let's see how we can implement this requirement in a declarative, reactive way.

Exploring the declarative pattern for filtering data

You should think of everything as a stream. This is the golden rule.

We have `recipes$`, which is our **data stream**. What if we were to consider the click on the **See results** button as a stream as well? We don't know when, but every time the user clicks on **See results**, the action stream emits the value of the filter.

In total, we have the data stream (responsible for getting the data) and the action stream (responsible for emitting the latest value of the filter). Both of the streams rely on each other; when `recipes$` emits a new value, the filter should stay active, and when the filter emits a new value, the recipes list should be updated accordingly.

What we are really trying to do is get information from different streams. And whenever you want to join information from multiple observables, you should think of one of the combination operators available in RxJS.

Instead of getting the data we need from both streams individually, we can combine it to form a single new stream. And when we have streams that rely on each other and particularly on the latest value emitted by each, we should think of the `combineLatest` operator.

The combineLatest operator

combineLatest will combine the latest values emitted by the input observables. So, every time one of the observables emits, combineLatest will emit the last emitted value from each. Does that make sense? If not, don't worry: we will detail it further by using a marble diagram as usual:

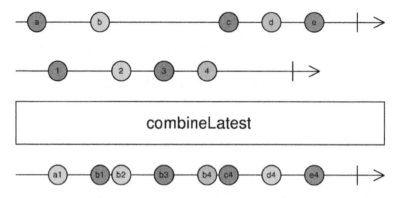

Figure 6.2 – The combineLatest marble diagram

Let's break this down:

- The first line in the marble diagram represents the timeline of the first input observable.

- The second line represents the timeline of the second input observable. So, combineLatest has two inputs.

- The last line represents the timeline of the output observable returned from the combineLatest operator.

Now let's dig deep into the execution.

The first observable emitted first the value **a**. At that time, the second observable had not emitted and nothing was emitted from combineLatest. Why? Because combineLatest **will not emit until all the input observables emit one value each**. So, when the second observable emits **1**, combineLatest will emit **a1**.

Bear in mind that combineLatest will not emit an initial value until each observable emits at least one value.

Then, the first observable emitted another value, which is **b**. At that time, the second observable had not emitted anything, but its last emitted value was **1**, so combineLatest will emit the last value of each, which is **b1**. Then, the second observable emitted **2**. At that time, the latest value emitted by the first observable was **b**, so combineLatest will emit **b2**, and so on and so forth.

The declarative pattern pillars

Let's come back to our example and see how we can combine the data stream and the action stream in order to filter results reactively.

The Recipesfilter component template remains unchanged. In the RecipesListComponent template, we will bind the [value] input of p-dataview to the array emitted from the newly created observable, filtredRecipes$:

- filtredRecipes$ should return all the recipes when loading the page.
- filtredRecipes$ should return the recipes that match the selected criteria when filtering.

The HTML code looks like this:

```
<div class="rp-data-view" *ngIf="filtredRecipes$ |async as
recipes" class="card">
    <p-dataView #dv [value]="recipes" [paginator]="true"
    [rows]="9" filterBy="name" layout="grid">
    /** Extra code here **/
    </p-dataView>
```

filtredRecipes$ will be the result of the combination of the data and action streams.

Now we will do the following:

1. Define the data stream.
2. Create the action stream.
3. Combine both of those streams.

Defining the data stream

Our data stream is recipes$, which we defined in RecipesListComponent as explained in *Chapter 4, Fetching Data as Streams*:

```
/*Define The data stream */
recipes$ = this.service.recipes$;
```

Creating the action stream

Now let's move on to the action stream, which will emit the criteria every time. We will create the action stream as follows in `RecipesService`:

```
/*Create The action stream */
Private filterRecipeSubject = new
  BehaviorSubject<Recipe>({title:''});
/* Extract The readonly stream */
filterRecipesAction$ =
  this.filterRecipeSubject.asObservable();
```

We can use either `Subject` or `BehaviorSubject` to create our action stream.

`Subject` is a special type of Observable that enables multicasting. We will explore multicasting in detail in *Chapter 8, Multicasting Essentials*. For now, keep in mind that a subject is an observer and an observable at the same time, so you can use it to share values among observers.

`BehaviourSubject` is a special type of subject that requires an initial value and always retains the last value to emit it to new subscribers. In other words, if you have any subscribers coming late to the game, they will get the last value emitted by the stream. This will always give you a value when you subscribe.

So, `filterRecipeSubject` is our action stream, which is a `BehaviorSubject` instance that has a default value defined in the constructor argument. In our case, it is an empty object. And I will tell you in a few moments why we use `BehaviorSubject` instead of a plain `Subject`.

The pattern we used here is as follows:

- Creating a **private** `BehaviorSubject` to prevent other parts of the code from calling the next, error, and complete methods on the `BehaviorSubject`. No external parts can emit values in the stream, error out, or complete the stream.

- Providing a read-only stream of our `filterRecipeSubject` so that the other parts of the app can subscribe to and get the data, which is `filterRecipeAction$`.

Combining the streams

Now it is time to combine the streams. And you may have guessed we will be using the `combineLatest` operator. Pass to it as a parameter an array of two values: the first one being the `recipes$` data stream and the second one being the `filterRecipeAction$` action stream. `combineLatest` will return an array of two values (as the number of input observables). The first element of the array is the last emitted value from the first stream and the second element of the array is the last emitted value from the second stream. It respects the order.

Let's create `filtredRecipes$` inside `RecipeListComponent` as follows:

```
filtredRecipes$ = combineLatest([this.recipes$,
  this.filterRecipesAction$])
```

But wait: we bound `filtredRecipes$` to our HTML template, remember? This stream should initially emit all the recipes, and when we click on **See results**, it should emit the filtered recipes.

This way, we can display in our UI all the recipes when loading the page and the filtered recipes when refining the results.

Therefore, we won't be returning the result of the combination directly. And in most cases, that won't happen anyway. Instead, we will process the result of the combination (the returned array), take the information that we need from the combined streams, and transform it into whatever we need.

In this case, we want to modify the result stream so that rather than just giving us the latest recipes and criteria values, it will give us an array of recipes filtered by the received criteria as follows:

```
filtredRecipes$ = combineLatest([this.recipes$,
  this.filterRecipesAction$]).pipe(
    map((resultAsArray: [Recipe[], Recipe]) => {
      return resultAsArray[0].filter(recipe =>
        recipe.title?.toLowerCase().indexOf(
        resultAsArray[1]?.title?.toLowerCase() ?? '') != -1)
    })
  );
```

The result of the combination is the `resultAsArray` parameter. The first element, `resultAsArray [0]`, represents the last emitted recipes from `recipes$`, and the second element, `resultAsArray [1]`, represents the last emitted criteria from `filterRecipesAction$`.

But we can do better! We can enhance the code using the array destructuring technique as follows:

```
filtredRecipes$ = combineLatest([this.recipes$, this.
filterRecipesAction$]).pipe(
    map(([recipes, filter]: [Recipe[], Recipe]) => {
      return recipes.filter(recipe =>
        recipe.title?.toLowerCase()
        .indexOf(filter?.title?.toLowerCase() ?? '') != -1)
    })
  );
```

Here, `recipes` represents the first element of the returned array and `filter` represents the second element of the returned array. After the `:`, we have the types, and that's it. So, instead of getting the elements by index directly, the array destructuring technique provides you with a way to name the array elements and get the values directly from those variables. Finally, we used the `filter` method to filter the list of recipes that match the criteria.

Emitting a value when an action occurs

This is the last step. As we said, every time the user clicks on the **See results** button, `filterRecipesAction$` should emit the criteria so that our `combineLatest` re-executes and returns the filtered recipes. To achieve this, we simply emit the last criteria when clicking on **See results** using the next method over the subject. The criteria are nothing but the form values. This is the code inside `RecipesFilterComponent`:

```
filterResults() {
    this.service.updateFilter(this.recipeForm.value);
}
```

And in `RecipesService`, we have this:

```
updateFilter(criteria:Recipe) {
  this.filterRecipeSubject.next(criteria);
}
```

On every emission of criteria, it will re-execute `combineLatest`. This is what the complete code looks like in `RecipesListComponent`:

```
import { ChangeDetectionStrategy, Component, OnDestroy, OnInit
} from '@angular/core';
import { RecipesService } from '../core/services/recipes.
service';
import { Recipe } from '../core/model/recipe.model';
import { map, takeUntil, tap } from 'rxjs/operators';
import { BehaviorSubject, combineLatest, Observable, Subject }
from 'rxjs';
import { FormBuilder } from '@angular/forms';


@Component({
  selector: 'app-recipes-list',
  templateUrl: './recipes-list.component.html',
  styleUrls: ['./recipes-list.component.scss'],
  changeDetection: ChangeDetectionStrategy.OnPush
})
export class RecipesListComponent implements OnInit {

  /*The data stream */
  recipes$ = this.service.recipes$;
  filtredRecipes$ = combineLatest([this.recipes$,
    this.filterRecipesAction$]).pipe(
    map(([recipes, filter]: [Recipe[], Recipe]) => {
      return recipes.filter(recipe =>
        recipe.title?.toLowerCase()
        .indexOf(filter?.title?.toLowerCase() ?? '') != -1)
      })
    );
```

```
  constructor(private service: RecipesService, private fb:
   FormBuilder) {
  }
}
```

RecipesFilterComponent looks like this:

```
export class RecipesFilterComponent implements OnInit {

  recipeForm = this.fb.group({
    title: [''],
    category: [''],
    ingredient: [''],
    tags: [''],
    prepTime: [''],
    cookingTime: [''],
  });

  constructor(private service: RecipesService, private fb:
   FormBuilder) { }

  ngOnInit(): void {
  }

  filterResults() {
    this.service.updateFilter(this.recipeForm.value);
  }

  clearFilter() {
  }
```

And finally, `RecipesService` looks like the following:

```
export class RecipesService {

  recipes$ = this.http.get<Recipe[]>(
   `${BASE_PATH}/recipes`);
  private filterRecipeSubject = new
   BehaviorSubject<Recipe>({ title: '' });
  filterRecipesAction$ =
   this.filterRecipeSubject.asObservable();

  constructor(private http: HttpClient) { }

  updateFilter(criteria:Recipe) {
     this.filterRecipeSubject.next(criteria);
  }

}
```

Now let's answer the question of why we should use `BehaviorSubject` instead of `Subject`.

When loading the page and before filtering or clicking on **See results**, we need `filtredRecipes$` to hold all the recipes as explained in the *Combine streams* section. If we use a plain `Subject`, the criteria will only get emitted when we click on the button. So, when loading the page, only `recipes$` emitted, and as we explained, `combineLatest` waits for all the streams to emit one value before starting emitting. In our UI, we will get an empty list.

However, when we use `BehaviorSubject`, it will emit the default value for all the subscribers immediately, so `combineLatest` will emit a first value, and everything will work fine and that's it. Seems like magic, right?

Here's an example of the filtered recipes when searching for Lemon as a keyword:

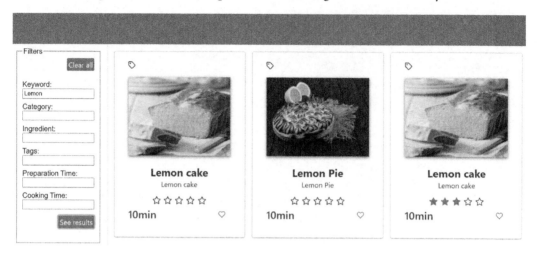

Figure 6.3 - Filtered recipes

To sum up, the following are the steps to resolve the use case we've looked at in this chapter:

1. Define the data stream.

2. Create the action stream.

3. Emit a value every time an action occurs.

4. Combine the action and data streams.

Summary

In this chapter, we explored one of the most commonly used RxJS patterns for filtering data, which can be used in many use cases. We learned about the `combineLatest` operator and how we can use it in implementing the reactive pattern. Then, we detailed the pillars of the declarative pattern and learned many useful techniques.

Now that we know about this useful pattern, let's move to the next reactive pattern, which is about transforming streams.

7

Transforming Streams

When dealing with streams, one of the most frequent use cases you will face is the need to transform a stream of certain values into a stream of other values. And this is what this chapter is about.

We will start by explaining the requirement that we will resolve by transforming streams. It is about implementing **autosave** behavior in the recipe app. Then, we will explore the imperative way of implementing this feature. Following that, we will learn the declarative pattern for doing it and study the most commonly used RxJS transformation operators for this situation.

In this chapter, we're going to cover the following main topics:

- Defining the requirement
- Exploring the imperative pattern for autosave
- Exploring the declarative pattern for autosave
- Learning about other useful higher-order mapping operators

Technical requirements

This chapter assumes that you have a basic understanding of RxJS.

For more details about Reactive forms, please refer to `https://angular.io/guide/reactive-forms`.

The autosave service used in this chapter and available in `recipes-book-api` is a fake used for demonstration purposes as the focus is not the backend.

The source code of this chapter, except for the samples, is available at `https://github.com/PacktPublishing/Reactive-Patterns-with-RxJS-for-Angular/tree/main/Chapter07`.

Defining the requirement

As described in the *View 2 – The new recipe interface* section of *Chapter 3, A Walkthrough of the Application*, the user can add a new recipe by clicking on the **New Recipe** menu item. This will display the following form to be filled out:

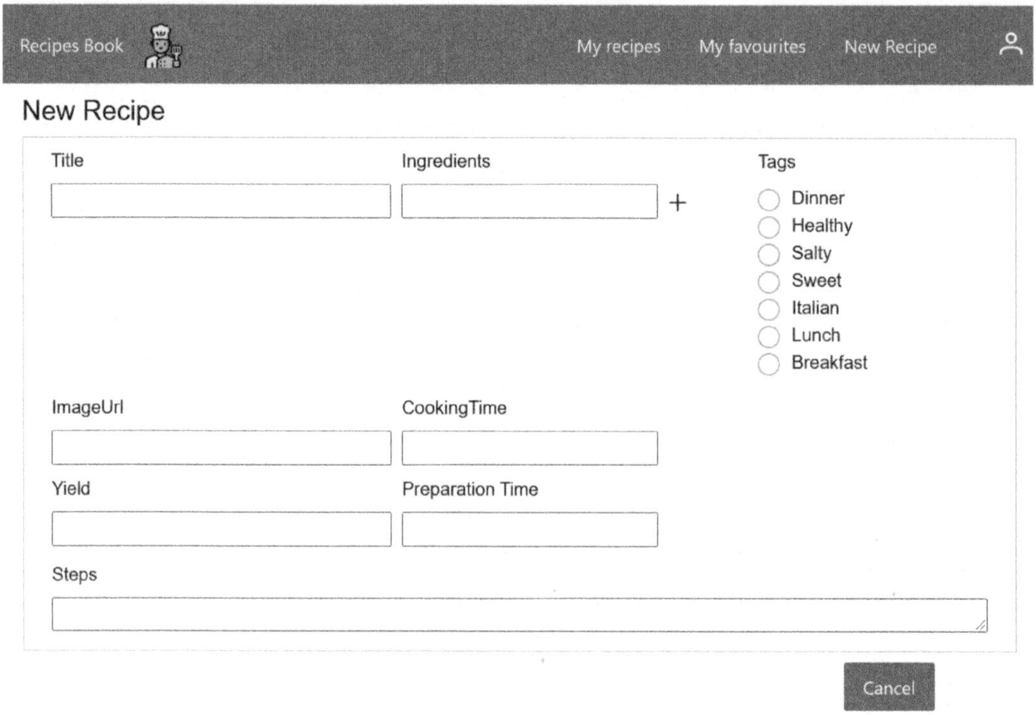

Figure 7.1 – The New Recipe form

The component responsible for displaying the **New Recipe** form is called `RecipeCreationComponent` and is available under `recipes-book-front\src\app\recipe-creation`. We want to implement autosave behavior, which consists of storing the user's changes in the form automatically. In this example, we will be storing the form changes in the backend, but they can also be stored on the client side; it all depends on the context. This feature improves the user experience by preventing data loss.

Now that we understand the requirement, let's look in the next section at the imperative way to implement autosave.

Exploring the imperative pattern for autosave

We used Angular Reactive forms to build the **New Recipe** creation form. As described in the *Using RxJS in Angular and its advantages* section of *Chapter 1, The Power of the Reactive Paradigm*, Reactive forms leverage RxJS by using the `valueChanges` observable to track the `FormControl` changes. This makes our jobs easier since we want to listen to the form's value changes in order to perform a save on every change. You can find the HTML code of the **New recipe** creation form in the `file recipe-creation.component.html` template.

In `recipe-creation.component.ts`, we only define the form as follows:

```
export class RecipeCreationComponent implements OnInit {

  constructor(private formBuilder: FormBuilder) { }

  recipeForm = this.formBuilder.group({
    id: Math.floor(1000 + Math.random() * 9000),
    title: [''],
    ingredients: [''],
    tags: [''],
    imageUrl: [''],
    cookingTime: [''],
    yield: [''],
    prepTime: [''],
    steps: ['']
  });
  tags = recipeTags.TAGS;
```

Please note that the formControl id is not going to be displayed in the form. We only create it to initialize the new Recipe object with a random identifier in order to save the new instance of the recipe properly in the backend.

The tags property is retrieved from a constant declared in src/app/core/model/tags.ts that represents the list of available tags.

The first thing that comes to mind to implement the autosave feature is subscribing to the valueChanges observable of recipeForm in the ngOninit() instance of our RecipeCreationComponent. Every time the valueChanges observable emits a new form value, we should perform a save request to save the most recent value of the form:

```
ngOnInit(): void {
    this.recipeForm.valueChanges
    .subscribe(
        formValue => {
            this.service.saveRecipe(formValue);
        }
    );
```

The saveRecipe method is defined and implemented in our RecipeService as follows:

```
saveRecipe(formValue: Recipe) : Observable<Recipe>   {
return    this.http.post<Recipe>(`${BASE_PATH}/recipes/save`,
formValue);
}
```

> **Note**
>
> The backend implementation is not the focus of this book. We provided a fake implementation of '/api/recipes/save' in the recipes-book-api project. The goal is simulating the call to an HTTP request to save the data.

The code of RecipeCreationComponent will look like this:

```
export class RecipeCreationComponent implements OnInit {


    constructor(private formBuilder: FormBuilder, private
    service: RecipesService) { }
```

```
recipeForm = this.formBuilder.group({
  id: Math.floor(1000 + Math.random() * 9000),
  title: [''],
  ingredients: [''],
  tags: [''],
  imageUrl: [''],
  cookingTime: [''],
  yield: [''],
  prepTime: [''],
  steps: ['']
});
tags = recipeTags.TAGS;


ngOnInit(): void {
  this.recipeForm.valueChanges
    .subscribe(
      formValue => {
        this.service.saveRecipe(formValue);
      }
    );


}


}
```

But this code won't work. You should know by now that the result of this.http.
post<Recipe>(`${BASE_PATH}/recipes/save`, formValue) is an
observable, and since observables are lazy, we should subscribe to it in order to initiate the
HTTP POST request. This way, we will fall, unfortunately, into the nested subscribes anti-
pattern, and the code will look like this:

```
ngOnInit(): void {
  this.recipeForm.valueChanges
    .subscribe(
      formValue => {
        this.service.saveRecipe(formValue).subscribe(
```

```
              result => this.saveSuccess(result),
              errors => this.handleErrors(errors)
        );
      }
    );
```

This implementation is problematic for several reasons:

- Every time we use `subscribe()`, we open the door to imperative code, and we have learned throughout this book that we should avoid that as much as we can.

- Nested subscriptions should be cleaned carefully; otherwise, we can run into various performance problems.

- We open up the possibility of serious timing issues. In fact, if multiple form values are emitted by `valueChanges` successively, many save requests will be sent in parallel. And if the requests take some time to complete, there is no guarantee that the backend will process the save requests in order. For instance, we cannot ensure that the last valid form value is indeed the one saved in the backend. Consequently, we will end up with data incoherence. What we really want to do is perform a save request after the previous one is completed.

So, let's see in the following section how we can implement this in a reactive and declarative way.

Exploring the reactive pattern for autosave

Let's think of the save operation as a stream; it is the result of the `this.service.saveRecipe(formValue)` method, which calls `this.http.post<Recipe>(`${BASE_PATH}/recipes/save`, formValue`. We will call it the `saveRecipe$` observable.

The `saveRecipe$` observable is responsible for saving the data in the backend. It will initiate the `http` request when subscribed to.

What we can do in this situation to avoid nested subscriptions is mapping or transforming the form value emitted by the `valueChanges` observable to the `saveRecipe$` observable. The result is what we call a higher-order observable. Not clear? Don't worry, we will explain this in detail in the next section. So, what is a higher-order observable? And how can it help us in this situation?

Higher-order observables

A higher-order observable is just an observable like any other, but its values are observables as well. In other words, it emits observables that you can subscribe to separately. OK, but when is it useful?

You can create a higher-order observable whenever you use data emitted from one observable to emit another observable. In our case, for every emitted form value from the valueChanges observable, we want to emit the saveRecipe$ observable. In other words, we want to transform or map the form value to the saveRecipe$ observable. This would create a higher-order observable where each value represents a save request. In this situation, the valueChanges observable is called the outer observable and saveRecipe$ is called the inner observable. We then want to subscribe under the hood to each saveRecipe$ observable emitted and receive the response all in one go to avoid nested treatments. The following figure illustrates my explanation:

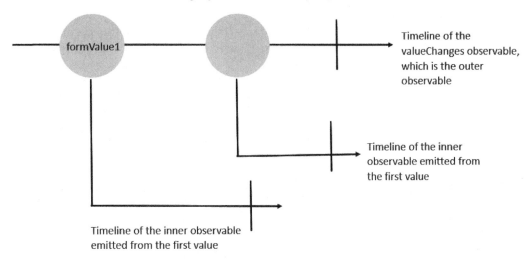

Figure 7.2 – The higher-order observable diagram

Now that we have learned what higher-order observables are and when to use them, let's focus on the higher-order mapping operators.

Higher-order mapping operators

In order to transform the outer observable, we should use higher-order mapping operators. The role of these operators is to map each value from an outer observable to a new inner observable and automatically subscribe and unsubscribe from that inner observable.

What is the difference between a higher-order mapping and a regular mapping?

Regular mapping involves mapping one value to another value. One of the most used basic mapping operators is the map operator:

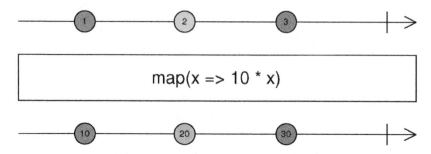

Figure 7.3 – The map operator – marble diagram

As described in this marble diagram, the map operator will transform the values of the input stream by multiplying each emitted value by 10. `x=>10*x` is the transformation function. This is how basic mapping works; higher-order mapping is about mapping one value into an observable.

RxJS provides several higher-order mapping operators. We will learn in the next section about the `concatMap()` operator, which we will use to implement the autosave behavior. Then, we will discover the other commonly used operators and the differences between them.

The concatMap operator

`concatMap` is the combination of the concatenation strategy and transformation (or mapping):

concatMap = concat (concatenation) + map (higher-order mapping)

We have already looked at the concepts of basic and higher-order mapping in the previous section.

Now let's look at the following marble diagram to understand the concatenation strategy. We will take the example of the `concat` operator:

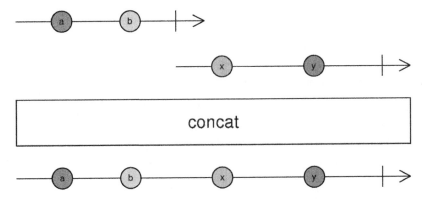

Figure 7.4 – The concat operator – marble diagram

- The first line represents the timeline of the first observable passed as input to the concat operator.

- The second line represents the timeline of the second observable passed as input to the concat operator.

- The concat operator in this example has two inputs. It will subscribe to the first observable but not to the second one. The first observable will emit the values **a** and **b**, which get reflected in the result observable (the last line).

- Then, the first observable completes, and at that moment, the concat operator subscribes to the second observable. This is how a sequential process is guaranteed.

- The second observable will emit the values **x** and **y**, which get reflected in the result observable.

- When the second observable completes, the output observable will also complete.

As you may have noticed, observable concatenation is all about observable completion. This is the key point. It emits the values of the first observable, waits for it to complete, and then emits the values of the next observable, and so on and so forth, until all the observables complete.

Now that we understand the concatenation strategy, we can define the concatMap operator as a mixture of higher-order mapping and observable concatenation: it waits for each inner observable to complete before processing the next one.

And the `concatMap` operator fits very well to our autosave requirement for the following reasons:

- We want to take the form value and turn it into a `saveRecipe$` observable and automatically subscribe and unsubscribe from the `saveRecipe$` inner observable — this is what a higher-order mapping operation does.

- We want to perform a save request only after the previous one is completed. When one HTTP save request is in progress, the other requests that come in the meantime should wait for its completion before getting called to ensure sequentiality. So, we need to concatenate the `saveRecipe$` observables together.

This is what the code will look like:

```
valueChanges$ = this.recipeForm.valueChanges.pipe(
  concatMap(formValue =>
   this.service.saveRecipe(formValue)),
  catchError(errors => of(errors)),
  tap(result=>this.saveSuccess(result))
);
```

Let's break down what is going on at the level of this code:

- Here, the outer observable, which is `valueChanges`, emits form values. For each emitted form value, `concatMap` transforms it to `this.service.saveRecipe(formValue)`, which is the `saveRecipe$` observable – our inner observable.

- `concatMap` automatically subscribes to the inner observable and the HTTP POST request will be issued.

- Another form value might come faster than the time it takes to save the previous form value in the backend. In this case, the form value will not be mapped to the `saveRecipe$` observable. Instead, `concatMap` will wait for the previous save request to return a response and complete before transforming the new form value to `saveRecipe$`, subscribing to it, and sending a new save request. When all inner observables complete, the result stream completes.

- Then, we use the `catchError` operator to handle the errors and register a side effect with the `tap` operator in order to log the message `Saved successfully` in the backend. You can customize this, of course, and display a message to the end user.

The complete code of `RecipeCreationComponent` will now look like this:

```
export class RecipeCreationComponent {


  constructor(private formBuilder: FormBuilder, private
    service: RecipesService) { }


  recipeForm = this.formBuilder.group({
    id: Math.floor(1000 + Math.random() * 9000),
    title: [''],
    ingredients: [''],
    tags: [''],
    imageUrl: [''],
    cookingTime: [''],
    yield: [''],
    prepTime: [''],
    steps: ['']
  });
  tags = recipeTags.TAGS;
  valueChanges$ = this.recipeForm.valueChanges.pipe(
    concatMap(formValue =>
      this.service.saveRecipe(formValue)),
    catchError(errors => of(errors)),
    tap(result=>this.saveSuccess(result))
  );



  saveSuccess(result: any) {
    console.log('Saved successfully');
  }
```

One thing is left: we should subscribe to the `valueChanges$` observable in order to make all of this work. And we will do so as usual through the async pipe in our template as follows:

```
export class RecipeCreationComponent {



  <ng-container *ngIf="valueChanges$ | async"></ng-
    container>
  /** All the form code here**/
```

Now the reactive implementation is complete. As you may have noticed, the first benefit of using `concatMap` is that now we no longer have nested subscriptions. We also get rid of explicit subscriptions thanks to the async pipe. Besides, all form values are going to be sent to the backend sequentially, as shown here in the Chrome Developer Tools **Network** tab:

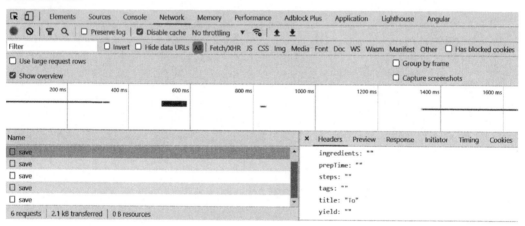

Figure 7.5 – Network tab

In order to avoid sending requests for every character introduced by the user, we can use the `debounceTime(waitingTime)` operator to wait for the user input to stabilize before sending the requests. We can optimize it further by ignoring duplicates, invalid values, and so on. This was an example of an implementation to dig deep into the `concatMap` operator.

> **Note**
>
> For more details about the `debounceTime` operator, please refer to
> `https://rxjs.dev/api/operators/debounceTime`.

To sum up, use `concatMap` when you want to ensure that operations are processed in sequence and each inner observable is processed one at a time and in order. There are other higher-order mapping operators that are useful in many situations. Let's talk about those operators in the next section.

Learning about other useful higher-order mapping operators

All higher-order mapping operators map each value from an outer observable to a new inner observable and automatically subscribe and unsubscribe from that inner observable. But not all operators adopt the `concat` strategy. There are different strategies, such as merge, switch, and exhaust. Let's break down those strategies!

The mergeMap operator

`mergeMap` is the combination of the merge and transformation (or mapping) strategies:

mergeMap = merge(merge) + map (higher-order mapping)

Now that you understand well the concepts of higher-order mapping, let's look at this marble diagram to understand the merging strategy. We will take the example of the `merge` operator:

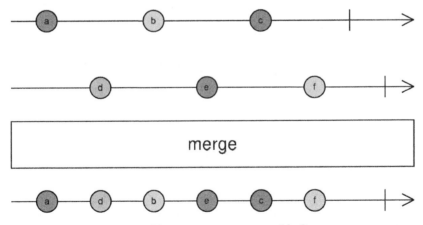

Figure 7.6 – The merge operator – marble diagram

Unlike `concat`, `merge` will not wait for an observable to complete before subscribing to the next observable. It subscribes to every inner observable at the same time and then outputs the values to the combined result. As described in this marble diagram, the values of the input observables are reflected in the output immediately. The result will not complete until all the merged observables complete.

mergeMap is a higher-order mapping operator that processes each inner observable in parallel.

Use mergeMap when you want to run operations in parallel. It enhances performance since each inner observable is processed concurrently, but only use mergeMap if the resulting order doesn't matter because it's possible that these requests will be processed out of order.

The switchMap operator

switchMap is the combination of the switch and transformation (or mapping) strategies:

switchMap = switch(switch) + map (higher-order mapping)

Let's look at the marble diagram of the switch operator to understand the switch strategy:

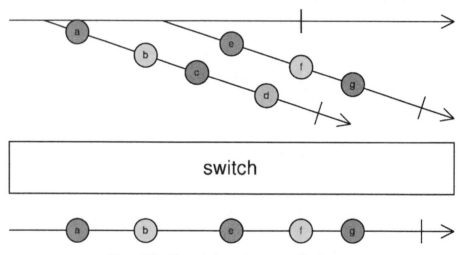

Figure 7.7 – The switch operator – marble diagram

Let's break down what is happening here. You are not used to seeing those diagonal lines, I know.

The top line is the higher-order observable. The higher-order observable emits the first inner observable (which has the values **a**, **b**, **c**, and **d**). The switch operator subscribes to it under the hood.

The first inner observable emits the values **a** and **b**, and they get reflected automatically to the resulting observable.

Then, the higher-order observable emits the second inner observable (which has the values **e**, **f**, and **g**).

The switch will unsubscribe from the first inner observable (**a-b-c-d**) and it subscribes to the second inner observable(**e-f-g**); that's why the values **e**, **f**, and **g** get reflected right after **a** and **b**.

As you may have noticed in switching, if a new observable starts emitting values, then the switch will subscribe to the new observable and unsubscribe from the previous one.

The switchMap operator is a higher-order mapping operator that unsubscribes from any prior inner observable and switches to any new inner observable. It is useful when you want to cancel an operation when a new one is triggered.

The exhaustMap operator

exhaustMap is the combination of the exhaust and transformation (or mapping) strategies:

exhaustMap = exhaust(exhaust) + map ()higher-order mapping

Let's look at this marble diagram to understand the exhaust strategy:

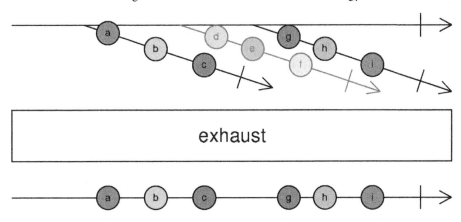

Figure 7.8 – The exhaust operator – marble diagram

The top line is a higher-order observable producing three inner observables over time. When the first inner observable (**a-b-c**) is emitted, exhaust will subscribe to it.

The values **a-b** get reflected in the output observable. Then, the second inner observable comes and gets ignored by the exhaust operator; it will not be subscribed to (this is the key part of exhaust).

Only when the first inner observable completes will exhaust subscribe to new observables.

So, the value **c** will get reflected, and the first inner observable completes. `exhaust` is ready now to treat other observables. At that point, the third inner observable comes. The switch will subscribe to and the values of the third inner observable, **g-h-i**, get reflected in the output.

`switchMap` is a higher-order mapping operator that unsubscribes from any prior inner observable and switches to any new inner observable.

In a nutshell, we can simply pick the right operator based on the use case:

- If the order is important and you need to process operations in sequence while waiting for completion, then `concatMap` is the right choice.

- If the order is not important and you need to process operations in parallel to enhance performance, `mergeMap` is the best operator.

- If you need to put a cancellation logic to release resources and take always the most recent information, then `switchMap` is the way to go.

- To ignore new observables while the current one is still ongoing, use `exhaustMap`.

Summary

In this chapter, we learned about the concepts of higher-order observables and higher-order mapping operators. We also learned about the `concat` strategy and how the `concatMap` operator works and how it can help us implement the autosave requirement in the recipe app in a reactive way. We focused on practical examples to better understand the concepts. Then, we explored other strategies, namely the use of the `merge`, `switch`, and `exhaust` higher-order mapping operators; we saw how each of them works and when and why to use each.

Let's move on to multicasting essentials in the next chapter.

Part 3 – Multicasting Takes You to New Places

In this section, you will understand the multicasting essentials in RxJS as well as the recommended reactive patterns in many multicasting use cases. Every use case will be endorsed by a real-world example.

This section comprises the following chapters:

8
Multicasting Essentials

Multicasting is one of the concepts that often confuses people at the first point when learning RxJS. But this concept is really useful and solves many problems in web applications.

In this chapter, I will demystify this concept for you and make it simple. We will start by explaining the difference between Multicasting and Unicasting, and then we will explore RxJS Subjects.

In this chapter, we're going to cover the following main topics:

- Explaining Multicasting versus Unicasting
- Exploring Subjects
- Highlighting the advantages of Multicasting

Technical requirements

This chapter assumes that you have a basic understanding of RxJS.

All the source code in this chapter is used for demonstration purposes as samples.

Explaining Multicasting versus Unicasting

Before hitting the concept of Multicasting, let's understand what Producer means.

Producer

Let's start by explaining the concept of Producer, which we will be using a lot in this chapter.

We call Producer the source of values of the Observable – for example, DOM events, WebSockets, and HTTP requests are regarded as Producers. Basically, it is any data source used to get values.

Observables basically fall into two types – hot and cold Observables. Let's understand the difference between them.

A cold observable

An observable is called cold when the data emitted is created by the Observable itself. The producer of the data is then created inside the observable itself. This is an example of a cold Observable:

```
import { Observable} from 'rxjs';


const coldObservable$ = new Observable(observer => {
  observer.next(Math.random());
  observer.next(Math.random());
  observer.complete();
});


/** First subscriber */
coldObservable$.subscribe(data => {
  console.log(`The first Observer : ${data}`);
});
```

```
/** Second subscriber */
coldObservable$.subscribe(data => {
  console.log(`The second Observer : ${data}`);
});

//console output
The first Observer: 0.043246216289945405
The first Observer: 0.7836505017199451
The second Observer: 0.18013755537578624
The second Observer: 0.23196314531696882
```

Let's break down what is happening in this code.

`Math.random()` is our Producer; it is called inside the Observable.

The first subscriber will get two random values after the subscription, and the second subscriber will get two different values after the subscription. In fact, every subscriber starts a new execution that implies a new call to `Math.random()`, which results in distinct values.

Each subscriber gets its own unique set of items. It begins to emit items only after the observer subscribes to it. Since there are two different executions, every observable will receive a different value. This means that data is unicast and not shared among the subscribers.

> **Note**
> A Unicast observable is an observable whose emitted values are not shared among subscribers.

So, for cold observables, the following applies:

- Data is produced by the Observable itself.
- It starts to emit data only after the observer subscribes to it.
- Each observer (or subscriber) gets its own unique set of items.

A hot observable

An observable is called hot when the data emitted is created outside the Observable. The producer of the data is created outside the observable itself. This is an example of a hot Observable:

```
import { Observable, fromEvent } from 'rxjs';
// Hot Observable
const hotObservable$ = fromEvent(document, 'click');


hotObservable$.subscribe(({ x, y }: MouseEvent) => {
  console.log(`The first subscriber: [${x}, ${y}]`);
});


hotObservable$.subscribe(({ x, y }: MouseEvent)=> {
  console.log(`The second subscriber: [${x}, ${y}]`);
});


//console output
The first subscriber: [108, 104]
The second subscriber: [108, 104]
```

Let's break down what is happening in this code.

We created an observable using the `fromEvent` function of RxJS. This Observable will emit clicks happening on the DOM document when subscribing to.

> **Note**
>
> For more details about `fromEvent`, please refer to `https://rxjs.dev/api/index/function/fromEvent`.

In this case, the data is emitted outside the Observable. And, as you may have guessed, both of the subscribers will get the same data. This means that the subscribers share the same instance of the DOM click event. So, the hot Observable shares data between multiple subscribers. We call this behavior Multicasting. In other words, the observable multicasts to all subscribers.

> **Note**
>
> A Multicast observable is an observable whose emitted values are shared among subscribers.

So, for hot observables, the following applies:

- Data is produced outside the Observable.

- It may begin emitting items as soon as it is created.

- The emitted items are shared between the subscribers (Multicasting).

If we want to transform the cold observable into hot, all we have to do is move the producer outside the observable and this way, our subscribers will receive the same data, as follows:

```
const value = Math.random();
const coldObservable$ = new Observable(observer => {
  observer.next(value);
  observer.next(value);
  observer.complete();
});


/** first subscriber */
coldObservable$.subscribe(data => {
  console.log(`The first subscriber: ${data}`);
});


/** second subscriber */
coldObservable$.subscribe(data => {
  console.log(`The second subscriber: ${data}`);
});


//console output
The first subscriber: 0.6642828154026537
The first subscriber: 0.6642828154026537
The second subscriber: 0.6642828154026537
The second subscriber: 0.6642828154026537
```

Is one more performant than the other? It really depends on the use case.

If you want to make sure multiple subscribers share the same data on each Observable, then you have to use hot observables.

The most frequently used ways to multicast values to observers in RxJS are RxJS Subjects and Multicasting operators.

Now that we have learned the difference between a cold and hot Observable and have a good understanding of Unicast and Multicast Observables, let's explore RxJs Subjects.

Exploring Subjects

Subjects are special types of Observables. While plain observables are Unicast, Subjects are Multicast. They allow Multicasting values to all the subscribers. You can regard Subjects as Observers and Observables at the same time:

- You can subscribe to Subjects to get emitted values by the Producer (that's why they act as Observables).

- You can send values, errors, and complete the stream using the next, error, and complete methods (that's why they act as an observer):

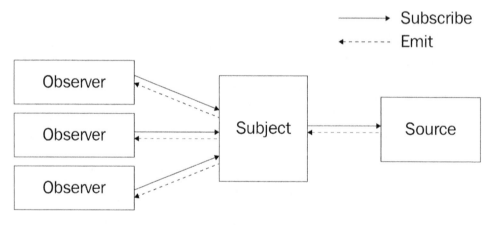

Figure 8.1 – An RxJS Subject

Remember that the Observer interface has the next, error and complete methods to, respectively, send values, error out, and complete an execution:

```
const observer = {
    next: x => console.log('Observer got a next value: ' +
                        x),
    error: err => console.error('Observer got an error:
                        '+err),
    complete: () => console.log('Observer got a completion'),
};
```

The Subject maintains a list of subscribers and notifies them when a new value is emitted. There are many types of Subjects; let's explore the most used ones.

A plain Subject

The plain Subject is the super class of all Subjects. Let's see a quick example:

```
const plainSubject$ = new Subject();
plainSubject$.next(10);
plainSubject$.next(20);

plainSubject$.subscribe({
    next: (message) => console.log(message),
    error: (error) => console.log(error),
    complete: () => console.log('Stream Completed'),
  });

plainSubject$.subscribe({
    next: (message) => console.log(message),
    error: (error) => console.log(error),
    complete: () => console.log('Stream Completed'),
  });


plainSubject$.next(30);

//console output
30
30
```

In the previous code, we created `plainSubject$`; the Subject sends 10 and '20' and after that we created two subscribers. Then, `plainSubject$` sends the value '30'. The subscribers only got the value '30'. So, what does it mean? This means that the subscribers will only get the values emitted after their subscription. What happened before their subscription was lost. This is how a regular Subject multicasts values.

If you want to keep a buffer of previous values to be emitted to subscribers coming late, then `ReplaySubject` can help with this!

ReplaySubject

`ReplaySubject` is a variant of a Subject. The following code explains how it works:

```
const replaySubject$ = new ReplaySubject();
replaySubject$.next(10);
replaySubject$.next(20);
replaySubject$.next(50);
replaySubject$.subscribe({
  next: (message) => console.log(message),
  error: (error) => console.log(error),
  complete: () => console.log('Stream Completed'),
});

replaySubject$.subscribe({
  next: (message) => console.log(message),
  error: (error) => console.log(error),
  complete: () => console.log('Stream Completed'),
});
replaySubject$.next(30);

//console output
10
20
50
10
20
50
30
30
```

As you saw, all the values were replayed to the new subscribers. In order to control the buffer size, you can pass it as a parameter when creating `ReplaySubject`:

```
const plainSubject$ = new ReplaySubject(2);
```

This will only replay the last two values, and the console output will be as follows:

```
20
50
20
50
30
30
```

Now, let's move on to the other variant of Subject – `BehaviorSubject`.

BehaviorSubject

`BehaviorSubject` is nothing but `ReplaySubject` with a buffer size equal to one, so it can replay only one previous item. `BehaviourSubject` requires an initial value and always retains the last value to emit it to new subscribers. In other words, if you have any subscribers coming late to the game, they will get the last value emitted by the stream. This will always give you value when you subscribe:

```
const behaviourSubject$ = new BehaviorSubject(1);
behaviourSubject$.next(10);
behaviourSubject$.next(20);
behaviourSubject$.next(50);


behaviourSubject$.subscribe({
  next: (message) => console.log(message),
  error: (error) => console.log(error),
  complete: () => console.log('Stream Completed'),
});


behaviourSubject$.subscribe({
  next: (message) => console.log(message),
  error: (error) => console.log(error),
  complete: () => console.log('Stream Completed'),
});
behaviourSubject$.next(30);


//console output
```

```
50
```
```
50
```
```
30
```
```
30
```

behaviourSubject$ created in this code has an initial value of 1.

behaviourSubject$ will emit the last value, 50, for new subscribers and then multicast the 30 value.

If no values were emitted when the subscriber came, then behaviourSubject$ will emit the default value, 1:

```
const behaviourSubject$ = new BehaviorSubject(1);


behaviourSubject$.subscribe({
  next: (message) => console.log(message),
  error: (error) => console.log(error),
  complete: () => console.log('Stream Completed'),
});


behaviourSubject$.subscribe({
  next: (message) => console.log(message),
  error: (error) => console.log(error),
  complete: () => console.log('Stream Completed'),
});
behaviourSubject$.next(30);
//console output
1
1
30
30
```

BehaviourSubject was used in *Chapter 6, Combining Streams*.

Plain Subjects, BehaviourSubject, and ReplaySubject are the most frequently used Subjects in RxJS. There are other types of Subjects, but they are used less, such as WebSocketSubject.

Highlighting Multicasting operators

There are many useful RxJS operators for Multicasting (or sharing values/executions) in RxJS 6, namely, `multicast`, `publish`, `share`, `shareReplay`, `publishReplay`, `publishLast`, and `refcount`. For more details about these operators, you can check the official docs: `https://rxjs.dev/api/operators`.

In version 7, Multicasting operators were consolidated to `share`, `connectable`, and `connect`. The other Multicasting APIs are now deprecated and will be deleted in RxJS 8. The only operator that wasn't deprecated is `shareReplay` because it is very popular. It is now a wrapper around the highly configurable `share` operator.

Since we are using RxJS 7 in this book, I think it is useless to go through all the deprecated operators. We will instead focus on the `share` operator, as it satisfies most cases. We will learn the behavior of the `share` operator by considering a real-world use case in the next chapter, *Chapter 9, Caching Streams*.

> **Note**
>
> For more details about RxJS 7 Multicasting operators, please refer to `https://rxjs.dev/deprecations/multicasting`.

Summary

In this chapter, I walked you through the most important concepts and vocabulary to understand Multicasting. We started by explaining the role of a Producer, and then we learned the difference between cold and hot Observables; this led us to the definition of Multicasting and Unicasting.

Finally, we explored RxJS Subjects, the different types of Subjects, and the use cases of each.

In the next chapter, we'll practice all of this in a real-world use case. We will learn how to put in place an efficient mechanism of caching in our Recipe app using Multicasting in RxJS and, more specifically, by combining Multicasting operators and Subjects.

9

Caching Streams

Caching data and assets is one of the most efficient ways to improve the user experience of our web applications. It is a good way to speed up the load times of our web applications and keep the number of network requests to a minimum.

We will start this chapter by defining the caching requirement for the client side and the motivation behind it. Then, we will learn how to implement this requirement in a reactive way and explore the useful operators in RxJS. After that, we will describe a better way to do it using RxJS 7. Finally, we will highlight the use cases of caching streams.

In this chapter, we're going to cover the following main topics:

- Defining the requirement
- Learning about using the reactive pattern to cache streams
- Exploring the RxJS 7 recommended pattern to cache streams
- Highlighting the use cases of caching streams

Technical requirements

This chapter assumes that you have a basic understanding of RxJS.

The source code of this chapter is available in `https://github.com/PacktPublishing/Reactive-Patterns-with-RxJS-for-Angular/tree/main/Chapter09`.

Defining the requirement

As you have learned throughout the previous chapters, the `HTTPClient` module is Observable-based, which means that methods such as `get`, `post`, `put` and `delete` return an Observable.

So, subscribing multiple times to this Observable will cause the source Observable to be re-created over and over again, hence performing a request on each subscription. It is a cold Observable, as we learned in *Chapter 8, Multicasting Essentials*. This behavior will result in an overhead of HTTP requests, which may decrease the performance of your web applications, especially if the server takes some time to respond.

Reducing HTTP requests by caching the result on the client side is one of the most commonly used techniques to optimize web applications. But when should we cache data? When data doesn't change frequently and it is used by more than one component, it makes a lot of sense to cache it and share it in multiple places. The user's profile data is a good example.

In the case of our `RecipesApp`, the `/api/recipes` GET request is called every time the `RecipesList` component is rendered in order to load the list of recipes. In other words, every time the user clicks on the recipe book logo or navigates between `HomeComponent` and `RecipeCreationComponent`, a GET request will be issued even if the list has not changed. This is what the **Network** tab in the Chrome console will look like:

Figure 9.1 – The GET HTTP requests overhead

As you may have noticed, all those outgoing requests are the result of the navigation between `HomeComponent` and the other components.

We will assume that the list of recipes does not change frequently. In this case, it is useless to request the server on every component's load; it would be better to cache the result and read the data from the cache to enhance the performance and the user experience. But what about updates? We absolutely won't force the user to reload the entire page just to get the most recent data from the server. Instead, we will configure an update interval to update the cache in the background so that the UI gets updated consequently.

Well, in a real-world application, we wouldn't refresh the data by requesting the server every interval (this technique is called **polling**). Instead, we will put in place a server push notification. But in this chapter, in order to understand the caching behavior in RxJS through basic examples, we will not use the push notification server to update the cache, which is an advanced technique; we will instead implement two simple types of cache:

- A static cache for static data that does not refresh
- A cache with refresh capacity

So, without further ado, let's look in the next section at how we can implement this.

Learning about using the reactive pattern to cache streams

What you will be glad to find is that RxJS ships with a very useful operator to put in place a caching mechanism for streams, which is the `shareReplay` operator.

The `shareReplay` operator shares an Observable execution with multiple subscribers. It has an optional parameter, which is `bufferSize`. Now, `bufferSize` represents the number of emissions that are cached and replayed for every subscriber. In our case, we only need to replay the most recent value; hence, we need to set the `bufferSize` parameter to 1.

In a nutshell, the `shareReplay` operator does the following:

- Shares an Observable execution with multiple subscribers

- Offers the possibility to replay a specified number of emissions to the subscribers

Our `recipes$` stream defined in `RecipesService` is initially a cold stream:

```
export class RecipesService {

  recipes$ = this.http.get<Recipe[]>(`${BASE_PATH}/recipes`);

}
```

This means that the stream's data is re-emitted for every subscriber, resulting in an overhead of HTTP requests. This is not what we want. We want to share the last stream's emission with all the subscribers, in other words, transforming the cold stream to a hot stream using the `shareReplay` operator as follows:

```
export class RecipesService {

  recipes$ = this.http.get<Recipe[]>(`${BASE_PATH}/recipes`).
pipe(shareReplay(1));
}
```

By passing 1 as an argument, `shareReplay` cached the `recipes$` last emission. But we can optimize further. The previous code will create a new cache instance for every subscriber. But what about sharing a single instance with all the subscribers? That would be much more performant. The following code illustrates the implementation:

```
export class RecipesService {

  recipes$ = this.getRecipesList();

  getRecipesList(): Observable<Recipe[]> {
    if (!this.recipes$) {
```

```
        return this.http.get<Recipe[]>(
          `${BASE_PATH}/recipes`).pipe(shareReplay(1));
    }
    return this.recipes$;
  }
}
```

Let's break down what is going on at the level of this code. We created a new method called getRecipesList() that will issue the HTTP request unless recipes$ is not defined. Then, we initialize recipes$ with the result of getRecipesList(). That's all!

Now let's explain the complete workflow:

1. The first time HomeComponent is initialized.

2. HomeComponent triggers the rendering of the child component: RecipesListComponent.

3. RecipesListComponent calls the recipes$ observable available in RecipeService, which will perform the GET HTTP request to retrieve the list of recipes since this is the first time we ask for the data.

4. Then, the cache will be initialized by the data coming back from the server.

5. The next time the data is requested, it will be retrieved from the cache.

Under the hood, the shareReplay operator creates a ReplaySubject instance that will replay the emissions of the source Observable with all the future subscribers. After the first subscription, it will connect the subject to the source Observable and broadcast all its values. This is the multicasting concept explained in *Chapter 8, Multicasting Essentials*.

The next time we request the recipes list, our cache will replay the most recent value and send it to the subscriber. There's no additional HTTP call involved. So, when the user leaves the page, it unsubscribes and replays the values from the cache.

This works perfectly fine when the data does not need to be refreshed at all. But as described in the requirement, we need to refresh RecipesList every interval. If the polling technique is used, then we can update the cache this way:

```
import { timer } from 'rxjs/observable/timer';
import { switchMap, shareReplay } from 'rxjs/operators';
const REFRESH_INTERVAL = 50000;
const timer$ = timer(0, REFRESH_INTERVAL);
```

```
export class RecipesService {

  recipes$ = this.getRecipesList();
  getRecipesList(): Observable<Recipe[]> {
    if (!this.recipes$) {
      return timer$.pipe(
      switchMap(_ =>
      this.http.get<Recipe[]>(`${BASE_PATH}/recipes`)),
      shareReplay(1)
    );
    }
    return this.recipes$;
  }
}
```

Let's break down what is happening at the level of this code. We created a `timer$` observable that will emit every 50 seconds. This interval is configured in the REFRESH_ INTERVAL constant. We used the `timer` function available in RxJS to create the `timer$` observable. For more details about the `timer` function, please refer to this link: `https://rxjs.dev/api/index/function/timer#examples`.

Then, for every emission, we use the `concatMap` operator to transform the value to the Observable returned by the HTTP client. This will issue an HTTP GET every 50 seconds and consequently update the cache. This is a known pattern using RxJS to execute a treatment every *x* seconds.

> **Note**
> If we use a push-based solution, then we can intercept the event of receiving messages to update the data.

Now let's see how we can customize the `shareReplay` operator.

With RxJS 6.4.0, a new signature was provided to allow configuring behavior when the operator's internal reference counter drops to zero. This is the contract of the `ShareReplayConfig` interface followed by the new signature of the `shareReplay` operator:

```
interface ShareReplayConfig {
  bufferSize?: number;
  windowTime?: number;
  refCount: boolean;
  scheduler?: SchedulerLike;
}
function shareReplay<T>(config: ShareReplayConfig):
MonoTypeOperatorFunction<T>;
```

When `refCount` is enabled (set to true), the source will be unsubscribed when the reference count drops to zero and the source will no longer emit. If `refCount` is disabled (set to false), the source will not be unsubscribed from, meaning that the inner `ReplaySubject` will still be subscribed to the source and potentially run forever.

To prevent surprises, it is highly recommended to use the signature that takes the `config` parameter this way:

```
shareReplay({bufferSize: 1, refCount: true })
```

So, the final code of `RecipesService` will look like this:

```
import { Injectable } from '@angular/core';
import { HttpClient } from '@angular/common/http';
import { BehaviorSubject, Observable, ReplaySubject, timer }
from 'rxjs';
import { Recipe } from '../model/recipe.model';
import { environment } from 'src/environments/environment';
import { shareReplay, switchMap } from 'rxjs/operators';
const BASE_PATH = environment.basePath
const REFRESH_INTERVAL = 50000;
const timer$ = timer(0, REFRESH_INTERVAL);

@Injectable({
  providedIn: 'root'
})
```

```
export class RecipesService {

  recipes$ = this.getRecipesList();
  private filterRecipeSubject = new
    BehaviorSubject<Recipe>({ title: '' });
  filterRecipesAction$ =
    this.filterRecipeSubject.asObservable();

  constructor(private http: HttpClient) { }

  updateFilter(criteria: Recipe) {
    this.filterRecipeSubject.next(criteria);
  }

  getRecipesList(): Observable<Recipe[]> {
    if (!this.recipes$) {
      return timer$.pipe(
      switchMap(_ =>
      this.http.get<Recipe[]>(`${BASE_PATH}/recipes`)),
        shareReplay({bufferSize: 1, refCount: true })
      );
    }
    return this.recipes$;
  }


  saveRecipe(formValue: Recipe): Observable<Recipe> {
    return this.http.post<Recipe>(
      `${BASE_PATH}/recipes/save`, formValue);
  }

}
```

Simple, right? Now that we know very well the behavior of shareReplay and all the useful options, let's explore a better way to do it using RxJS 7 in the next section.

Exploring the RxJS 7 recommended pattern to cache streams

A lot of work was done in version 7 to consolidate multicasting operators. The `multicast`, `publish`, `publishReplay`, `publishLast`, and `refCount` operators were deprecated and will be removed in RxJS 8.

The only operators remaining are `shareReplay`, `share`, and `connectable`. And the `share` operator **rules them all**, meaning that it is highly recommended to use the `share` operator instead of `Connectable` and `shareReplay` in most cases. The `shareReplay` operator is too popular to deprecate but may be deprecated in future versions as there is an alternative to it, especially because `shareReplay`, when not used carefully, can cause memory leaks, particularly with infinite streams.

The `share` operator is enhanced in version 7 with an optional configuration object as an argument, which makes it more flexible and ready to do the job of other operators.

In this `share` configuration object, you can choose the subject you're connecting through and define your reset behavior. And this is how we can achieve the behavior of the `shareReplay` operator using the `share` operator:

```
getRecipesList(): Observable<Recipe[]> {
    if (!this.recipes$) {
      return this.http.get<Recipe[]>(
        `${BASE_PATH}/recipes`).pipe(share({
        connector : () => new ReplaySubject(),
        resetOnRefCountZero : true,
        restOnComplete: true,
        resetOnError: true
      }));
    }
    return this.recipes$;
}
```

If you're using version 7 of RxJS, it is highly recommended to call the `share` operator instead of `shareReplay`. The preceding code has the same behavior as the `shareReplay` operator.

Highlighting the use cases of caching streams

The first use case is optimizing the HTTP requests in order to enhance the performance of our web applications. All that you have to do is put the result in a cache that is a shared place for all the consumers. This is what we did in the previous section.

There is another use case where caching streams makes a lot of sense: when accounting for expensive side effects on the streams. In general, we call the actions that we perform after a value is emitted side effects. This could be logging, displaying messages, doing a kind of mapping, and so on. Here's an example of a side effect using the `tap` operator:

```
import {map, from } from 'rxjs';
import { tap } from 'rxjs/operators';

const stream$ = from([1, 2, 'Hello', 5]);
stream$

  .pipe(
    tap((value) => console.log(value)),
    map((element) => {
      if (isNaN(element as number)) {
        throw new Error(element + ' is not a number');
      }
      return (element as number) * 2;
    })
  )
  .subscribe({
    next: (message) => console.log(message),
    error: (error) => console.log(error),
    complete: () => console.log('Stream Completed'),
  });

//console output
1
2
2
4
Hello
Error
```

In this code, we are performing a transformation for every number emitted; we multiply it by 2 and return the multiplied value. If the value is not a number, an error is thrown. But we need to log the initial value before the transformation. That's why we called the `tap` operator before the `map` operator to log the original value. This is a basic example of a side effect, but it could be also handling errors or displaying messages.

> **Note**
>
> For further details about the `tap` operator, please refer to the official documentation: `https://rxjs.dev/api/operators/tap`.

In some situations, the side effects can perform actions more complex than logging, displaying messaging and handling errors. Some side effects perform some computations that represent an expensive treatment in terms of performance. Unfortunately, those treatments will be executed by every subscriber, even though it is enough to execute them only once. Otherwise, it will harm the performance of your application.

If you have this use case in your application, then it is highly recommended to use the `share` operator to cache the result and execute heavy treatments only once.

Summary

In this chapter, we explained the concepts of caching in web applications, including its benefits and use cases. We focused on a concrete example in our recipes app, detailed the requirement, and implemented it in a reactive way. We learned about the behavior of the `shareReplay` operator and the alternative implementation using the `share` operator in RxJS 7. We also learned how to implement a static cache and a cache with refresh capacity. Finally, we highlighted the most common use cases of caching.

In the next chapter, we will explore another useful reactive pattern that allows you to share data between your components. As usual, we will demystify the concepts and then learn the reactive way to do it.

10
Sharing Data between Components

Sharing data between components is a very common use case in web applications. Angular provides many approaches to communicate between parent and child components, such as the popular @Input and @Output decorator patterns. The @Input() decorator allows a parent component to update data in a child component. The @Output() decorator, on the other hand, allows the child component to send data to a parent component. That's great, but when data needs to be shared between components that are either deeply nested or not immediately connected at all, those kinds of techniques become less efficient and difficult to maintain.

So, what's the best way to share data between sibling components? This is the heart of this chapter. We will start by explaining our requirement; then we will walk you through the different steps to implement the reactive pattern for sharing data between sibling components. Finally, we will highlight the other alternatives for sharing data and handling your application's state.

In this chapter, we're going to cover the following main topics:

- Defining the requirement
- Exploring the reactive pattern to share data
- Highlighting other ways of sharing data

Technical requirements

This chapter assumes that you have a basic understanding of RxJS.

The source code of this chapter is available at `https://github.com/ PacktPublishing/Reactive-Patterns-with-RxJS-for-Angular/tree/ main/Chapter10`.

Defining the requirement

Let's assume that we have components (**C1**, **C2**, **C3**, and **C4**) that do not have any relationship with each other and there is information (**DATA**) shared between those components:

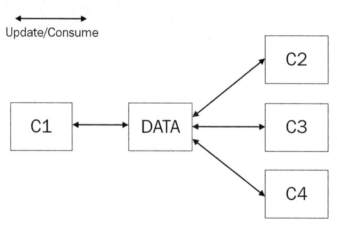

Figure 10.1 – Shared data between components

The components can update **DATA** and consume it at the same time. But at any time during the process, the components should be able to access the last value of **DATA**.

Well, this is the requirement in an abstract way. Let's make it clearer with a concrete example.

In our `RecipeApp`, when the user clicks on one recipe, it gets selected, and we want all the components to have access to the last-selected recipe by the user.

Exploring the reactive pattern to share data

Angular services are powerful and efficient for creating common references for sharing both data and business logic between components. We will combine Angular services with Observables, more specifically `BehaviorSubject`, to create stateful, reactive services that will allow us to synchronize the state efficiently across an entire application. So, in the following subsections, let's explain the steps to implement a reactive pattern to share data between unrelated or sibling components.

Step one – creating a shared service

We will create an Angular service called `SharedDataService` using the Angular CLI, as usual under the `src/app/core/services` folder:

```
ng g s SharedData
```

In the `SharedDataService` class, we need to create the following:

- A `private BehaviorSubject` called `selectedRecipeSubject` to multicast the value of the currently selected recipe, which represents the data to be shared. It is a strongly typed `BehaviorSubject`. The type of its emissions will be `Recipe`. We initialize it with an `empty` object as the default value, since initially, we don't have any selected value. We define the `selectedRecipeSubject` value as `private` to protect it from external use; otherwise, any external process could call the next method and change the emissions, which is dangerous:

  ```
  private selectedRecipeSubject = new
  BehaviorSubject<Recipe>({});
  ```

- A `public` observable that is extracted from `selectedRecipeSubject` to handle data as an observable. We used the `asObservable()` method available in the `Subject` type. The emissions of this observable are consumed in read-only mode. External processes can only consume its emissions, not change them:

  ```
  selectedRecipeAction$ =
  this.selectedRecipeSubject.asObservable();
  ```

- Finally, we need to define a method that will update the shared data, which is the selected recipe. This method only calls next on selectedRecipeSubject to notify all subscribers of the last-selected recipe passed as a parameter. The process that updates the selected recipe will call this method:

```
updateSelectedRecipe(recipe: Recipe) {
    this.selectedRecipeSubject.next(recipe);
}
```

This is what the service looks like after putting all the pieces together:

```
import { Injectable } from '@angular/core';
import { BehaviorSubject } from 'rxjs';
import { Recipe } from '../model/recipe.model';

@Injectable({
  providedIn: 'root'
})
export class SharedDataService {

  private selectedRecipeSubject = new
    BehaviorSubject<Recipe>({});
  selectedRecipeAction$ =
    this.selectedRecipeSubject.asObservable();

  updateSelectedRecipe(recipe: Recipe) {
    this.selectedRecipeSubject.next(recipe);
  }

  constructor() { }
}
```

Step two – updating the last-selected recipe

We should update the shared selectedRecipe instance when the user clicks on one of the recipe cards in the dashboard:

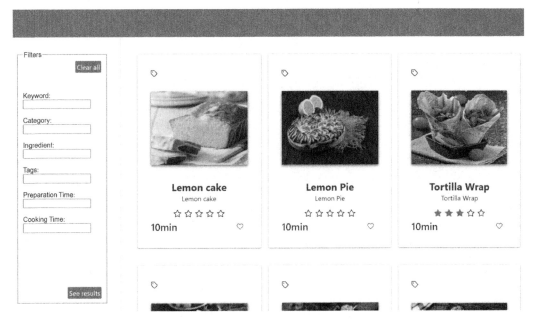

Figure 10.2 – The list of recipes

So, in order to update the shared `selectedRecipe` when the user clicks on the card, we have to add the `(click)` output that calls the method that will perform the update. In our case, it is the `editRecipe(recipe)` method. This is the HTML code snippet:

```
<div class="rp-data-view" *ngIf="filtredRecipes$ |async as
recipes" class="card">
    <p-dataView #dv [value]="recipes" [paginator]="true"
    [rows]="9" filterBy="name" layout="grid">
        <ng-template let-recipe pTemplate="gridItem">
            <div class="p-col-12 p-md-3">
                <div style="cursor: pointer;"
                (click)="editRecipe(recipe)" class=
                "recipe-grid-item card">
            </div>
        </div>
        </ng-template>
    </p-dataView>
</div>
```

In `RecipesListComponent`, we implement the `editRecipe` method, which takes as input the selected recipe and performs two actions:

- It updates the last-selected recipe by calling `updateSelectedRecipe(recipe:Recipe)`, which we created in `SharedDataService`. So, we should inject the `SharedDataService` service in `RecipesListComponent`.

- It displays the details of the recipe in `RecipeDetailsComponent`:

```
editRecipe(recipe: Recipe) {
    this.sharedService.updateSelectedRecipe(recipe);
    this.router.navigate(['/recipes/details']);
}
```

Step three – consuming the last-selected recipe

In the `RecipeDetails` component, we need to consume the last-selected recipe in order to display the details of the last-selected recipe. So, again, we need to inject `SharedDataService` and subscribe to the `selectedRecipeAction$` public observable, which will emit the last-selected recipe, as follows:

```
export class RecipeDetailsComponent implements OnInit {

    constructor(private sharedService: SharedDataService) { }
    selectedRecipe$ =
      this.sharedService.selectedRecipeAction$;

    ngOnInit(): void {
    }

}
```

That's it! This is how you can share data between unrelated components throughout the application.

Now, we can use the latest value of the recipe everywhere. We only have to inject `SharedDataService` into the component that needs the shared data and subscribe to the public Observable that represents the read-only value. We can, for example, add this code in `HeaderComponent` to display the title of the last-selected recipe in the application's header:

```
<div *ngIf="selectedRecipe$ | async; let recipe">
    <span> {{recipe.title}} </span>
</div>
```

So, if we change the shared value in any of the components, all the other components will get notified to update their processes.

We used this pattern in *Chapter 6, Combining Streams,* to share the value of the filter in `RecipesFilterComponent` with `RecipesListComponent`, and then we combined the streams to display the filtered results.

To summarize everything, here's a visual representation of the reactive pattern steps:

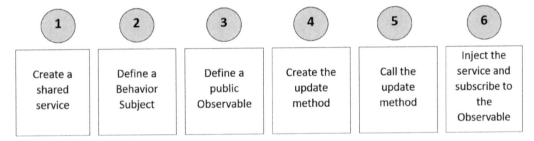

Figure 10.3 – The GET HTTP requests overhead

1. Create a shared Angular service.

2. Define a private `BehaviorSubject` that will multicast the shared value to the subscribers. You need to specify the type of it, and it should be initialized with the default value of the shared data. As we use `BehaviorSubject`, late subscribers will always get the last value emitted, since `BehaviorSubject` stores the last-emitted value. Each `consumer` component should access the same copy of the data. `BehaviorSubject` here is only handled inside the shared service.

3. Define a public Observable that will hold the read-only shared value.

4. Create the `update` method inside the service that will update the shared value by calling the `next` method in the `Subject` type and passing the last value.

5. Inject the service in the component that *updates* the value of the shared data and call the `update` method implemented in the service (*step 4*).

6. Inject the service in the component that *consumes* the value of the shared data and subscribe to the exposed Observable in the service.

As far as I'm concerned, this is the simplest way to share data between unrelated components in Angular. But there are better ways for more complex scenarios; let's highlight them in the next section.

Highlighting other ways for sharing data

The previous pattern for sharing data has many benefits:

- Improves the sharing of data between unrelated components

- Manages mutability risk

- Makes communication between components easier

We can use Angular services and RxJS's `BehaviorSubject` to manage our application's state. This works perfectly in many situations, but for big applications where there are a lot of user interactions and multiple data sources, managing states in services can become complicated.

In this case, we can use a state management library to manage the state of our application, which is the main goal of state management libraries.

There are many great state management libraries out there to manage states in Angular. The most popular is NgRx. All the state management libraries have one thing in common – they are built on top of RxJS Observables and the state is stored in `BehaviorSubject`.

> **Note**
>
> For further details about NgRx, please refer to `https://ngrx.io/guide/store`.

Summary

In this chapter, we explained the motivation behind sharing data between components and learned how to implement it in a reactive way. We learned how we can use `BehaviorSubject` combined with `AngularServices` to share data between unrelated components and manage our application state. Finally, we went through the alternatives of state management for more complex scenarios. This will help you put in place a good architecture for your web application, which will make it more reactive, more performant, and reduce the cost of maintainability.

In the next chapter, we will explore the pattern of bulk operations.

11
Bulk Operations

Bulk operations are tasks performed on a large scale, such as uploading many files, deleting many items in one shot, and assigning recipes to the same category on a mass scale. We will start by explaining the requirement and the type of bulk operation that we will consider, and then we will walk you through the different steps to implement the reactive pattern for implementing bulk operations. Finally, we will learn about the reactive pattern for tracking progress.

In this chapter, we're going to cover the following main topics:

- Defining the requirement
- Learning about the reactive pattern for bulk operations
- Learning about the reactive pattern for tracking progress

Technical requirements

This chapter assumes that you have a basic understanding of RxJS.

The source code of this chapter is available at `https://github.com/PacktPublishing/Reactive-Patterns-with-RxJS-for-Angular/tree/main/Chapter11`.

Defining the requirement

In the UI, the bulk operation is represented by one action or event. In the background, there are two possible behaviors, whether running one network request for all the tasks or running parallel network requests for every task.

In this chapter, we want to allow the user to upload the recipe images in one shot, track the progress of the upload operation, and display this progress to the user:

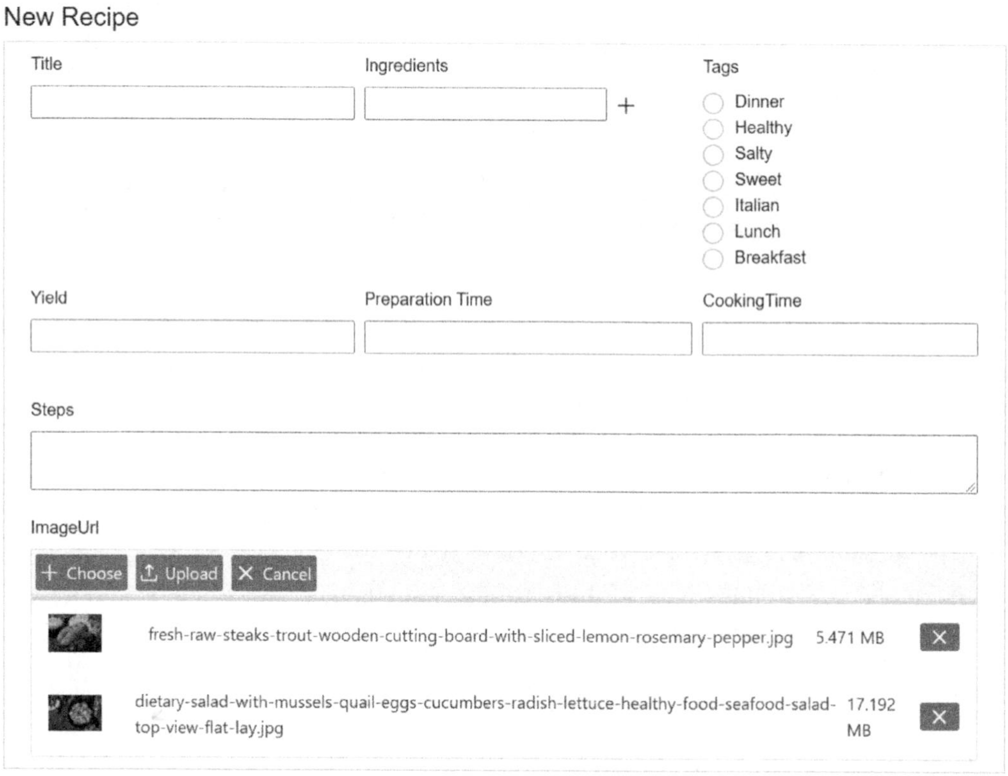

New Recipe

Figure 11.1 – Upload the recipe's images

In the `RecipeCreation` interface, we changed the layout of the **ImageUrl** field to the **File Upload** layout available in our library of components, PrimeNG. The **File Upload** layout allows the user to choose multiple files, clear the selection, and upload the files.

The upload is done on the server, and we have a specific service for the upload that takes the file to be uploaded as input and the identifier of the associated recipe to this file. Since the backend upload API supports only one file at a time, we will be running N network requests in parallel to uploading N files. This is the bulk change use case that we will consider in this chapter.

In the UI, we have one event that will trigger multiple requests at the same time. The following diagram provides a graphical representation of the bulk operation:

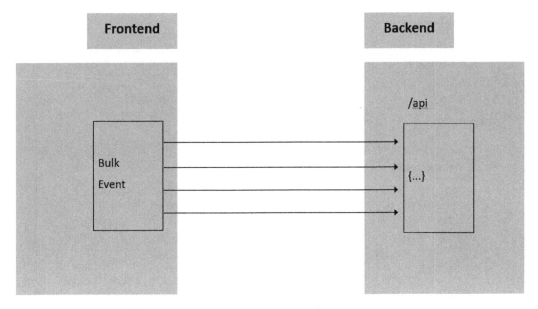

Figure 11.2 – A bulk operation visualization

To sum up, we want to do the following:

- Allow the user to upload many files after clicking only one time on the upload button.

- Display the progress of this bulk operation.

Now that we have defined the requirement, let's learn in the next section how we can implement it in a reactive way.

Learning about the reactive pattern for bulk operations

We have to consider as usual our tasks as streams. The task that we are going to perform is uploading the recipe image in the backend. So, let's imagine a stream called `uploadRecipeImage$` that will take the file and the recipe identifier as input and perform an HTTP request. If we have N files to be uploaded, then we will create N streams.

We want to subscribe to all those streams together, but we are not interested in the values emitted from each stream through the process; we only care about the final result (the last emission), whether the file is uploaded successfully, or whether something wrong happens and the upload fails.

Is there an RxJS operator that gathers a list of Observables together to get a cumulative result? Yes, thankfully, we have forkJoin. Let's understand the role and behavior of this operator.

The forkJoin operator

The forkJoin operator falls under the category of combination operators. If we look at the official documentation, we find this definition:

> *Accepts an Array of ObservableInput or a dictionary Object of ObservableInput and returns an Observable that emits either an array of values in the exact same order as the passed array, or a dictionary of values in the same shape as the passed dictionary.*

In other words, forkJoin takes a list of streams as input, waits for the streams to complete, and then combines the last values they emitted in one array and returns it. The order of the values in the array is the same as the order of the input Observables.

Let's consider the following marble diagram, as usual, to better understand:

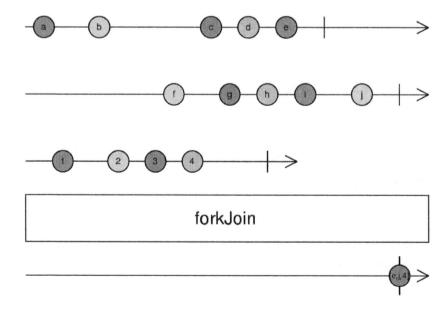

Figure 11.3 – A forkJoin marble diagram

`forkJoin` has three input Observables (consider the three timelines before the operator box).

The first Observable emitted the **a** value; `forkJoin` does not emit anything (look at the last timeline after the operator box, which represents the returned result by `forkJoin`).

Then, the third Observable emitted **1** and, again, nothing was emitted by `forkJoin`. Why? Because, as we said in the definition, `forkJoin` will emit only once when all the Observables are complete.

So, as illustrated in the marble diagram, `forkJoin` emitted only once at the same time the last Observable (the second one) was completed. The first Observable (represented by the first timeline) was completed first, and the last value emitted was **e**. Then, the third Observable (represented by the third timeline) was completed, and the last value emitted was **4**. At that time, `forkJoin` did not emit any value because there was still an Observable running.

Finally, the last Observable (represented by the second timeline) was completed, and the last value emitted was **j**. Therefore, `forkJoin` returns an array containing the results of each stream in the order of the input Observables (**e**, **j**, and **4**).

The order of completion is not considered; otherwise, we would have had `[e,4,j]`. Even though the third Observable was completed before the second one, `forkJoin` respected the order of the input Observables and returned the **j** value before the **4** value.

So, keep in mind that `forkJoin` emits once when all the input Observables are complete and preserves the order of the input Observables.

This fits our requirements so well! `forkJoin` is best used when you have a list of Observables and only care about the final emitted value of each. In our case, we will issue multiple upload requests, and we only want to take action when a response is received from all the input streams.

Let's see the pattern in action.

The pattern in action

First, we need to create `UploadRecipesPreviewService` under `src/app/core/services`, which is responsible for uploading the files. Here is the code of the service:

```
import { HttpClient } from '@angular/common/http';
import { Injectable } from '@angular/core';
import { Observable } from 'rxjs';
import { environment } from 'src/environments/environment';
```

```typescript
import { UploadStatus } from '../model/upload.status.model';
const BASE_PATH = environment.basePath

@Injectable({
  providedIn: 'root'
})
export class UploadRecipesPreviewService {

  constructor(private http: HttpClient) { }
  /**
   * Uploads the file
   * @param code
   * @param fileToUpload
   * @returns
   */
  upload(code: string, fileToUpload?: File):
  Observable<UploadStatus> {
    const formData = new FormData()
    formData.append('fileToUpload', fileToUpload as File)
    return this.http.post<UploadStatus>(
      `${BASE_PATH}/recipes/upload/${code}`,
      formData
    )
  }
}
```

The upload method issues the upload HTTP request and returns the upload status. It takes as input two parameters:

- code: The identifier of the recipe
- fileToUpload: The file to be uploaded

Then, we need to implement the behavior of the **Upload** button. For this purpose, in the `RecipeCreationComponent` template, we need to specify the method that will be called when clicking on the **Upload** button. We named the `onUpload` method in our case and put it as a value to the callback (`uploadHandler`), provided by the component library we are using.

Here's the HTML template snippet:

```
<div class="form-row">
  <div class="col-12">
    <label for="ImageUrl">ImageUrl</label>
    <p-fileUpload name="imageUrl" [multiple]=true
     [customUpload]="true" (uploadHandler)=
     "onUpload($event?.files)">
    </p-fileUpload>
  </div>
</div>
```

The link to the full code of the template is mentioned in the *Technical requirements* section.

The following step is implementing the `onUpload(event: any)` method that is called when clicking on the **Upload** button.

We will create `BehaviorSubject`, which will always emit the last value of the uploaded files called `uploadedFilesSubject$`. We initialize it with an empty array:

```
uploadedFilesSubject$ = new BehaviorSubject<File[]>([]);
```

In the `onUpload` method, we send the last array of the uploaded files to `uploadedFilesSubject$`, as follows:

```
onUpload(files: File[]) {
   this.uploadedFilesSubject$.next(files);
}
```

Now, we should create the stream responsible for doing the bulk upload that we called `uploadRecipeImages$`, as follows:

```
uploadRecipeImages$ = this.uploadedFilesSubject$.pipe(
  switchMap(uploadedFiles=>forkJoin(uploadedFiles.map((
    file: File) =>
  this.uploadService.upload(this.recipeForm.value.id,
    file))))
)
```

Let's break down what's going on at the level of this code, piece by piece.

Every time we click on the **Upload** button, `uploadedFilesSubject$` will emit the files to be uploaded. We need to subscribe to `uploadedFilesSubject$` and use the transformation technique using `switchMap`, which we learned about in *Chapter 7, Transforming Streams*.

We use `switchMap` to transform every value emitted by `uploadedFilesSubject$` to the Observable that we will build using `forkJoin`. The `forkJoin` operator should take the array of streams that will be combined as input. That's what we did inside `forkJoin`.

We map every file in the `uploadedFiles` array to the stream responsible for uploading the file, and the stream responsible for uploading the file is nothing but the following instruction:

```
this.uploadService.upload(this.recipeForm.value.id,
  file))))
```

This is simply the call to the `upload` method available in `UploadRecipesPreviewService` that takes `id` (which we retrieved from `recipeForm`) and the file as input.

So, we will have an array of Observables that we will pass as input to `forkJoin`, and that's it!

Finally, we need to inject `UploadRecipesPreviewService` in the constructor and subscribe to `uploadRecipeImages$` in the template, as follows:

```
<ng-container *ngIf="uploadRecipeImages$ | async"></ng-
container>
```

Now, let's suppose one of the inner streams errors out. The `forkJoin` operator will no longer emit any values for us. This is another important thing to be aware of when using this operator. You will lose the value of any other stream that would have already been completed if you do not catch the error correctly on the inner Observable. Therefore, catching the error in this case is crucial!

This is how we handle it:

```
uploadRecipeImages$ = this.uploadedFilesSubject$.pipe(
  switchMap(uploadedFiles=>forkJoin(uploadedFiles.map((
    file: File) =>
  this.uploadService.upload(this.recipeForm.value.id,
    file).pipe(
    catchError(errors => of(errors)),

  ))))
```

We called `catchError` on the inner stream returned by the `upload` method. Then, we wrapped the error inside another Observable and returned it. This way, the `forkJoin` stream will stay alive.

If you are only interested in all inner Observables completing successfully, then you can catch the error on the outside.

It makes a lot of sense to catch the errors in order to display something significant to the user – for example, in our case, if one of the uploads fails because `maxFileSize` was reached or the extension of the image is not allowed, then the system should display those exceptions to the user to help them fix the file.

To sum up, `forkJoin` has the following benefits:

- It is very useful when you are interested in combining results and getting a value only once.
- It only emits once when all the Observables complete.
- It preserves the order of the input Observables in the emission.
- It will complete when one of the streams errors out, so, you should handle the error.

So far, so good. This works nicely, but what if we need to know some information during the process, such as how many files were already uploaded? What is the progress of the operation? How much time do we still need to wait? With the current `forkJoin` implementation, it is not possible, but let's see in the next section how we can do it.

Learning about the reactive pattern for tracking progress

In order to track the progress of the bulk upload, we can call a very useful operator called `finalize`. The `finalize` operator allows you to call a function when the Observable completes or errors out.

The idea is to call the `finalize` operator and execute a function that will calculate the progress. This way, every time an Observable completes, the progress will get updated. This is what the code will look like:

```
counter: number = 0;
uploadProgress: number=0;


uploadRecipeImages$ = this.uploadedFilesSubject$.pipe(
    switchMap(uploadedFiles =>
     forkJoin(uploadedFiles.map((file: File) =>
      this.uploadService.upload(this.recipeForm.value.id,
       file).pipe(
        catchError(errors => of(errors)),
         finalize(() => this.calculateProgressPercentage(
          ++this.counter, uploadedFiles.length))
       ))))
    )


    private calculateProgressPercentage(completedRequests:
     number, totalRequests: number) {
      this.uploadProgress =
       (completedRequests/totalRequests)*100;
    }
```

The `finalize` operator calls the `calculateProgressPercentage` private function, which takes the following parameters:

- **The number of completed requests**: We just declare a property counter that we will increment every time the Observable completes.

- **The total number of requests**: This number is retrieved from the array of `uploadedFiles`.

Inside the `calculateProgressPercentage` function, we just perform a simple computation and store the result in an `uploadProgress` property.

Then, you can map the value of this property to any `ProgressBar` component in the UI. This way, you will be able to display the progress to the user.

Summary

In this chapter, we explained the concept of bulk operation and learned how to implement a real-world example of a bulk task in a reactive way. We learned the behavior and a use case of the `forkJoin` operator and went through the different steps to implement a bulk upload. Finally, we went through the tracking progress functionality and how we can implement it using a reactive technique.

In the next chapter, we will explore the pattern of real-time updates and the different techniques available in RxJS to implement them at the lowest cost.

12
Processing Real-Time Updates

Real time is a very hot topic nowadays. The demand for *real-time* features has been growing in web applications. So, how can you process real-time messages in the frontend and update the displayed data automatically in the UI? This is what we will cover in this chapter. We will start by explaining the requirement, and then we will walk you through the different steps to implement the reactive pattern for consuming real-time updates. Finally, we will learn the reactive pattern for handling reconnection.

In this chapter, we're going to cover the following main topics:

- Defining the requirement
- Learning the reactive pattern for consuming real-time messages
- Learning the reactive pattern for handling reconnection

Technical requirements

This chapter assumes that you have a basic understanding of RxJS.

We used the ws library, which is a WebSocket Node.js library, in order to support WS in our backend. For more details, you can check out this link: `https://github.com/websockets/ws`.

The source code of this chapter is available at `https://github.com/PacktPublishing/Reactive-Patterns-with-RxJS-7-in-Angular-applications/`.

Defining the requirement

There are two techniques available for publishing real-time data on the web:

- **Pull technique**: This is where the client raises a request to get the latest version of data. **HTTP polling** and **HTTP long polling** are two examples of implementations of the pull technique.

- **Push technique**: This is where the server pushes updates to the client. **WebSockets** and **Server Sent Events** are two implementations of the push technique.

In general, push techniques have a lower latency compared to pull ones. We are not going to dive into these techniques in detail and compare them, as it is not the goal of this chapter. However, we will use the WebSocket technology for our requirement.

In short, the WebSocket protocol is a stateful communication protocol that establishes a low-latency bidirectional communication channel between a client and a server. This way, messages can be sent back and forth between the server and the client. The following diagram illustrates the WebSocket communication flow:

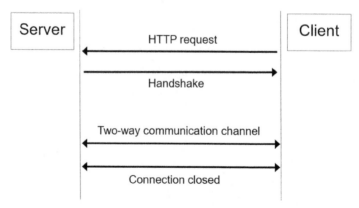

Figure 12.1 – WebSocket communication

As illustrated in the preceding figure, there are three steps in WebSocket communication:

1. **Opening the connection**: In this step, the client issues an HTTP request to tell the server that a protocol upgrade will occur (from HTTP to WebSocket). If the server supports WebSockets, then the protocol switch will be accepted.

2. **Establishing the communication channel**: Once the protocol upgrade is done, then a bidirectional communication channel will be created, and messages start to be sent back and forth between the server and the client.

3. **Closing the connection**: When the communication is over, a request will be issued to close the connection.

At this level, that is all that you need to know about WebSockets. You will find a ready-to-use WebSocket backend under the `recipes-book-api` folder that pushes notifications to the client.

Now that we have highlighted the different techniques available for implementing a real-time feature and learned the basics of the WebSocket protocol, let's explore in the next section the reactive pattern for consuming real-time messages. We want to consume the live updates sent by the WebSocket server and update the UI automatically without having to trigger a **Refresh** button.

Learning the reactive pattern for consuming real-time messages

RxJS has a special type of Subject called `WebSocketSubject` that allows you to communicate with a WebSocket server. Let's learn about the behavior of this Subject and its capabilities.

The WebSocketSubject behavior

`WebSocketSubject` is nothing but a wrapper around the W3C WebSocket object available in the browser. It allows us to both send and consume data through a WebSocket connection.

The WebSocketSubject creation

In order to use WebSocketSubject, you have to call the webSocket factory function that produces this special type of Subject and takes the endpoint of your WebSocket server as input. The following is the function signature:

```
webSocket<T>(urlConfigOrSource: string |
WebSocketSubjectConfig<T>): WebSocketSubject<T>;
```

It accepts two types of arguments: either a string representing the URL of your endpoint or a special object of the WebSocketSubjectConfig type that contains the URL of your endpoint, along with other properties. We will explore WebSocketSubjectConfig in detail in the *Learning the reactive pattern for handling reconnection* section.

The following is an example of calling the webSocket factory function with the first type of argument:

```
import { webSocket } from "rxjs/webSocket";
const subject = webSocket("ws://localhost:8081");
```

The following is an example of calling the webSocket factory function with the second type of argument:

```
import { webSocket } from 'rxjs/webSocket';
const subject$ = webSocket({url:'ws://localhost:8081'});
```

In our case, the URL of our endpoint is ws://localhost:8081. You can use ws for a secure WebSocket connection (which is the same as HTTPS for a secure HTTP connection).

Opening the connection

Now that you have a reference of WebSocketSubject, you should subscribe to it in order to establish the connection with your ws endpoint and start receiving and sending data:

```
import { webSocket } from 'rxjs/webSocket';
const subject$ = webSocket({url:'ws://localhost:8081'});
subject$.subscribe();
```

If you don't subscribe, the connection will not be created.

Listening to incoming messages from the server

As WebSocketSubject is nothing but a regular RxJS Subject, you can register callbacks to process the incoming messages from the WebSocket server.

In order to listen to messages, you should subscribe to the produced WebSocketSubject from the webSocket factory function and register a callback, as follows:

```
const Subject$ = webSocket('ws://localhost:8080');

// Listen to messages from the server
const subscription1 = Subject$.subscribe(msg => {
    console.log('Message received from the socket'+ msg);
});
```

Pushing messages to the server

In order to send messages to the server, we can use the next method available in the subject type, as follows:

```
// Push messages to the server
subject$.next('Message to the server')
```

Handling errors

You can also catch errors coming from the server using catchError as usual and push errors to the server by calling the error method. But bear in mind that when you send an error, the server will get notified about this error, and then the connection will be closed. So, nothing will get emitted thereafter:

```
// Push errors to the server
subject$.error('Something wrong happens')

// Handle incoming errors from the server
subject$.error('Something wrong happens')
```

Closing the connection

You can use `unsubscribe` or `complete` to close the connection:

```
// Close the connection
subject$.complete();
//or
subject$.unsubscribe();
```

As you may have noticed, only the creation of `WebSocketSubject` is specific to this special kind of Subject. All the other APIs used are the same as those used for regular Subjects. So, there is nothing fancy here.

The following figure illustrates the whole process:

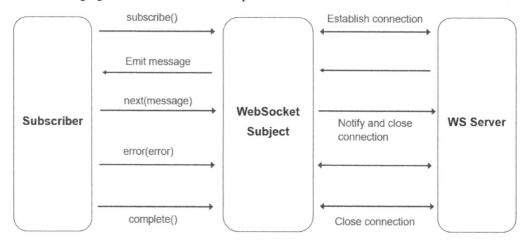

Figure 12.2 – WebSocketSubject possible events

Connection management

If the same instance of `WebSocketSubject` has many subscribers, then they will share the same connection to save resources. However, if we have two different instances of `WebSocketSubject`, it will establish two distinct connections, even if they are referencing the same endpoint. Be aware of this behavior! The following code explains the connection management for both use cases:

```
const firstSubject$ = webSocket('ws://localhost:8080');
const  secondSubject$ = webSocket('ws://localhost:8080');

// the first subscriber, opens the WebSocket connection
```

```
const subscription1 = firstSubject$.subscribe(msg => {
});
// the second subscriber, uses the already opened WebSocket
    connection
const subscription2 = firstSubject$.subscribe(msg => {
});
//this subscriber opens a new connection
const subscription3 = secondSubject$.subscribe(msg => {
});
```

Let's explain what's happening in this code. We create two instances of
WebSocketSubject called firstSubject$ and secondSubject$ respectively
that reference the same ws endpoint. Then, we create a subscription to the
firstSubject$; this first subscription will open the WebSocket connection. Then,
we create a second subscription to the same Observable, firstSubject$; this second
subscription will use the already opened WebSocket connection.

However, the subscription to secondSubject$ will open a new WebSocket connection.
Why? Because it is a new reference to the WebSocket Subject, even though it references
the same ws endpoint as firstSubject$.

Now, if we have many subscribers sharing the same connection and one of those
subscribers decides to complete, then the connection will be released unless there are no
more subscribers listening, as described in the following code block:

```
const subject$ = webSocket('ws://localhost:8080');
// the first subscriber, opens the WebSocket connection
const subscription1 = subject$.subscribe(msg => {});


// the second subscriber, uses the already opened WebSocket
    connection
const subscription2 = subject$.subscribe(msg => {});


// the connection stays open
subscription1.unsubscribe();


// closes the connection
subscription2.unsubscribe();
```

This is all that you need to know to make a basic scenario work. Simple, right? Now, let's see the recommended pattern to put in place our Recipes app.

Putting the pattern into action

Now that we know how to create a connection to our ws endpoint, it is time to explore the different steps to consume real-time messages. The first step is isolating all the interactions with WebSocketSubject in a separate Angular service.

Step one – creating a real-time service

We will create an Angular service called RealTimeService under src/app/core/ services. In this service, we will start by creating the following:

1. A private property, socket$, that will contain the reference to the WebSocket Subject that we will create in the getNewWebSocket() method.

2. A private method, getNewWebSocket(), that returns WebSocketSubject produced by the webSocket factory function that takes WS_ENDPOINT as input. WS_ENDPOINT is a constant that contains the value of the wsEndpoint property available in the environment file. The URL of the endpoints can change from one environment to another. That's why it is recommended to put that information in the environment files.

3. A public method, sendMessage(), that sends a message given as input to the socket, which will forward the message to the server.

4. A public method, close(), that closes the connection by completing the Subject.

This is how the code of RealTimeService will look after putting all these pieces together:

```
import { Injectable } from '@angular/core';
import { webSocket, WebSocketSubject } from 'rxjs/webSocket';
import { environment } from '../../../environments/
environment';
import { Observable, EMPTY, BehaviorSubject } from 'rxjs';
import { tap, switchAll, catchError } from 'rxjs/operators';
import { Message } from '../model/message.model';
export const WS_ENDPOINT = environment.wsEndpoint;
export const RECONNECT_INTERVAL = environment.
reconnectInterval;
@Injectable({
```

```
    providedIn: 'root'
})
export class RealTimeService {

    private socket$!: WebSocketSubject<Message> | undefined;
    public getNewWebSocket(): WebSocketSubject<Message> {
        return webSocket(WS_ENDPOINT);
    }

    sendMessage(msg: Message) {
        this.socket$?.next(msg);
}
    close() {
        this.socket$?.complete();
    }
}
```

Then, we will add the `connect()` method that will listen to the incoming messages in a reactive way:

```
public connect(): void {
  if (!this.socket$ || this.socket$.closed) {
  this.socket$ = this.getNewWebSocket();
  const messages = this.socket$.pipe(
  tap({
            error: error => console.log(error),
        }), catchError(_ => EMPTY));
    }
  }
```

Let's break down what is going on in this method. If `socket$` is undefined (not yet created) or closed, then `socket$` will be populated by the newly produced `WebSocketSubject` from the `getNewWebSocket` method. Then, we will combine the `tap` and `catchError` operators to handle errors. The `tap` operator is used to log a message when an error occurs or when the connection closes.

The `catchError` operator handles errors and returns an empty Observable. The returned Observable from the pipe operation will be stored in a constant called `messages`.

So far, so good! Now, we will create a private Subject named `messagesSubject$` that will emit the messages Observable (the messages observable returned from the socket). So, it is an Observable of Observables:

```
private messagesSubject$ = new
BehaviorSubject<Observable<Message>>(EMPTY);
public connect(): void {
  if (!this.socket$ || this.socket$.closed) {
  this.socket$ = this.getNewWebSocket();
  const messages = this.socket$.pipe(
  tap({
          error: error => console.log(error),
        }), catchError(_ => EMPTY));
      this.messagesSubject$.next(messages);
    }
  }
```

After that, we will provide a read-only copy from the `messagesSubject$` observable through the `messages$` public Observable. We used the `SwitchAll` operator to flatten the Observable of Observables:

```
private messagesSubject$ = new
BehaviorSubject<Observable<Message>>(EMPTY);
public messages$ = this.messagesSubject$.pipe(switchAll(),
catchError(e => { throw e }));
public connect(): void {
  if (!this.socket$ || this.socket$.closed) {
  this.socket$ = this.getNewWebSocket();
  const messages = this.socket$.pipe(
  tap({
          error: error => console.log(error),
        }), catchError(_ => EMPTY));
      this.messagesSubject$.next(messages);
    }
  }
```

We will be subscribing to messages$ in every component that needs to consume real-time updates.

Why do we do this?

The idea is to protect Subject$ and the incoming messages from any external update and expose the messages as read-only to the external components and services. This way, any component interested in consuming the real-time messages has to subscribe to messages$, and all the logic related to the socket will be handled privately in this service.

Step two – triggering the connection

After putting the server in place, we should call the connect method from our root component because we want it to be called only once:

```
constructor(private service: RealTimeService ) {
this.service.connect();
}
```

Step three – defining the Observable emitting live updates

Then, we call the messages$ Observable in the Angular component that consumes the live updates:

```
liveData$ = this.service.messages$.pipe(
  map(rows => rows.message),
  catchError(error => { throw error }),
  tap({
    error: error => console.log('[Live component] Error:',
     error),
    complete: () => console.log('[Live component]
    Connection Closed')
  }
  )
);
```

As you can see in the preceding code snippet, in our case, we process the incoming messages from the server and transform the current Observable – map(rows => rows.message). We handle the errors using the catchError and tap operators, and then the result is stored in the liveData$ Observable.

Step four – subscribing to the Observable emitting live updates

Now, we are one step from displaying the live data; we just have to subscribe to the `liveData$` Observable in our component's template using the async pipe.

And we are done!

Step five – changing detection strategy

In case of frequent updates in the UI, it is highly recommended to set the change detection strategy to `onPush` in order to optimize the performance:

```
changeDetection: ChangeDetectionStrategy.OnPush
```

That's it! You will be able to consume live updates in a reactive way using this pattern.

At this point, you may be wondering how to handle reconnection. When the server is restarted or the connection crashes for whatever reason, does this Subject restore the lost connection under the hood? The answer is *no*. The reconnection capability is not provided by `WebSocketSubject`.

But you can implement this easily in your web application using RxJS. Let's learn how you can do this in the next section.

Learning the reactive pattern for handling reconnection

When the connection to the WebSocket server is lost, the channel will be closed, and `WebSocketSubjet` will no longer emit values. This is not the expected behavior in the real-time world. The reconnection capability is a must in most cases.

Therefore, let's imagine, for example, that after a disconnection, a system tries to reconnect after every 3 seconds. The solution, in this case, is intercepting the closure of the socket and retrying the connection. How can we intercept the closure of the connection?

This is possible thanks to `WebSocketSubjectConfig`, which is responsible for customizing some behavior in the socket life cycle. The following is the API:

```
export interface WebSocketSubjectConfig<T> {
  url: string;
  protocol?: string | Array<string>;
  openObserver?: NextObserver<Event>;
  serializer?: (value: T) => WebSocketMessage;
```

```
deserializer?: (e: MessageEvent) => T;
closeObserver?: NextObserver<CloseEvent>;
closingObserver?: NextObserver<void>;
WebSocketCtor?: { new(url: string,
  protocols?:string|string[]): WebSocket };
binaryType?: 'blob' | 'arraybuffer';
}
```

The properties of WebSocketSubjectConfig previously described are ones that you can customize, namely the serialization and deserialization methods. The closure and opening of the connection…

The full description of each property is available at the official documentation link: http://bit.ly/RxJS-WebSocket.

In order to benefit from WebSocketSubjectConfig, you should call the webSocket factory function that takes the second type of parameter. The following code creates WebSocketSubject using WebSocketSubjectConfig and simply intercepts the closure event to display a custom message:

```
public getNewWebSocket(): WebSocketSubject<Message> {
    return webSocket({
      url: WS_ENDPOINT,
      closeObserver: {
        next: () => {
          console.log('[DataService]: connection closed');
        }
      },
    })
  }
```

Now that we know how to intercept the closure of the connection, let's learn how to retry the reconnection.

Retrying the reconnection

We can combine the `retryWhen` operator that resubscribes to an Observable conditionally after it completes with the `delayWhen` operator that sets the delay between two consecutive connections.

Let's create a function that will retry to connect to a given Observable every configurable `RECONNECT_INTERVAL`. We will log in to the browser's console on every attempt at reconnection:

```
private reconnect(observable: Observable<Message>):
Observable<Message> {
return observable.pipe(retryWhen(errors => errors.pipe(tap(val
=> console.log('[Data Service] Try to reconnect', val)),
delayWhen(_ => timer(RECONNECT_INTERVAL))))));
}
```

This `reconnect` function will be used as an RxJS custom operator to handle the reconnection after the socket's closure in the `connect()` method of our `RealTimeService`, as follows:

```
public connect(cfg: { reconnect: boolean } = { reconnect: false
}): void {

  if (!this.socket$ || this.socket$.closed) {
    this.socket$ = this.getNewWebSocket();
    const messages = this.socket$.pipe(cfg.reconnect ?
    this.reconnect : o => o,
      tap({
        error: error => console.log(error),
      }), catchError(_ => EMPTY))
    this.messagesSubject$.next(messages);
  }
}
```

As you can see, a new Boolean `reconnect` parameter is added to the `connect` function to differentiate between the reconnection and the first connection. This optimizes the code and avoids adding an additional function.

Then, all you have to do is call the connect function with reconnect: true when intercepting the connection closure, as follows:

```
public getNewWebSocket(): WebSocketSubject<Message> {
  return webSocket({
      url: WS_ENDPOINT,
      closeObserver: {
        next: () => {
            console.log('[DataService]: connection closed');
            this.socket$ = undefined;
            this.connect({ reconnect: true });
        }
      },
   })
  }
```

This way, after the connection closure, you will see many outgoing requests from the client trying to reach the server every 3 seconds.

The reconnection capability is a must in the real-time world. This is how we handled it using RxJS in a few lines of code. Many developers don't know that RxJS offers this feature that enables you to consume real-time messages coming from WebSocket and add many third-party libraries to handle this requirement, while it is also available out of the box. So choosing RxJS, in this case, is one less dependency!

Summary

In this chapter, we implemented a real-world example of consuming real-time messages coming from a WebSocket server in a reactive way. We explained the requirement and the context. Then, we explored the features of WebSocketSubject and learned how we can consume real time messages through the WebSocketSubject and how this special kind of Subject works. Finally, we learned how we can build a reconnection mechanism in a reactive way using WebSocketSubjectConfig and the RxJS operators.

Now, it is time to learn how we can test the reactive patterns that we have built so far using RxJS, which we will see in the next chapter.

Part 4 – Final Touch

In this section, we will explore the different testing strategies to secure our Patterns

This section comprises the following chapters:

- *Chapter 13, Testing RxJS Observables*

13

Testing RxJS Observables

Many developers consider testing observables a challenging task. This is true. But if you learn the right techniques, you can implement maintainable and readable tests in a very effective manner.

In this chapter, we will walk you through three commonly used patterns for testing streams. We will start by explaining the **subscribe and assert** pattern, after which we will discuss the **marble testing** pattern. Finally, we will highlight a suitable pattern for testing streams that are returned from `HTTPClient` by focusing on a concrete example in our Recipe app.

In this chapter, we're going to cover the following main topics:

- Learning about the subscribe and assert pattern
- Learning about the marble testing pattern
- Highlighting testing streams using the HTTPClient module

Technical requirements

This chapter assumes that you have a basic understanding of RxJS. Angular is where we will be testing observables. This chapter assumes that you have a basic understanding of unit testing in Angular using **Jasmine**: `https://angular.io/guide/testing`.

The unit test for the `saveRecipe` method, which is available in the `RecipesService` class, will be available in `recipes.service.spec`.

The source code for this chapter is available at `https://github.com/PacktPublishing/Reactive-Patterns-with-RxJS-7-in-Angular-Applications`.

Learning about the subscribe and assert pattern

As we have learned so far, observables are lazy and we don't get any value until we subscribe to them. In tests, it is the same thing – observables will not emit any value until we subscribe to them. To solve this, programmers always tend to subscribe to the observables manually inside the tests.

Let's suppose we have to test a method called `getValue(value: boolean)` that's available in an Angular service called `SampleService`. This method is very simple: it returns an observable that will emit the Boolean value that's given as input, as follows:

```
export class SampleService {


  getValue(value: boolean): Observable<boolean> {
    return of(value);
  }


}
```

The test of this method will look like this:

```
describe('SampleService', () => {
  let service: SampleService;
  beforeEach(() => {
    service = TestBed.inject(SampleService);
  });

```

```
    it('should return true as a value', () => {
        service.getValue(true).subscribe(
        result=>expect(result).toEqual(true))
    });
});
```

Let's explain what is happening in this code. We start by defining our group of specs/the test suite using `describe()`. Then, we inject `SampleService` into the `beforeEach` statement to provide a shared instance of the service that we will be using in all the specs. Finally, we define the test case or spec of our `getValue(value: boolean)` method. Inside the spec, we subscribe to the `getValue(true)` method and expect the result to be equal to `true` since we passed the `true` value as input. Now, let's run `ng test`; the test passes and everything is fine:

```
TOTAL: 2 SUCCESS
√ Browser application bundle generation complete.
Chrome 95.0.4638.69 (Windows 10): Executed 2 of 8 (skipped 6) SUCCESS (0.046 secs / 0.018 secs)
TOTAL: 2 SUCCESS
√ Browser application bundle generation complete.
Chrome 95.0.4638.69 (Windows 10): Executed 2 of 8 (skipped 6) SUCCESS (0.046 secs / 0.016 secs)
TOTAL: 2 SUCCESS
√ Browser application bundle generation complete.
Chrome 95.0.4638.69 (Windows 10): Executed 1 of 7 (skipped 6) SUCCESS (0.038 secs / 0.018 secs)
TOTAL: 1 SUCCESS
```

Figure 13.1 – ng test output

Quite simple, right? This is a positive scenario.

Now, let's handle a negative scenario to see whether the tests are working properly or not. To do so, we will replace `true` with `false` in the assertion:

```
    it('should return true as a value', () => {
    service.getValue(true).subscribe(
    result=>expect(result).toEqual(false))
    });
```

Let's run `ng test`. While we are expecting our test to fail, it is passing! How is this possible?

The thing with expectations in testing is that if you have an unmatched expectation, it throws an error. And if you have an unhandled error inside an RxJS subscription, it will be thrown on a separate call stack, meaning that it is asynchronously thrown. Therefore, tests that use the subscribe and assert pattern will be green even though, in reality, they are failing.

To overcome this, we should pass a done callback to the test function and call it manually after our expectations when the test has been completed, as follows:

```
it('should return true as a value', (done) => {
  service.getValue().subscribe(
  result=>expect(result).toEqual(false))
 done();
});
```

This way, our tests will work as expected. So, don't forget to call the done callback! Otherwise, in an asynchronous scenario, the test may finish and be valid without actually checking our assertion. The done callback tells the testing framework when the test is done and makes your tests more resilient. It is supported by many testing frameworks such as Jasmine, Jest, and Mocha, so you should be pretty good with this approach.

Now, let's consider a more complicated method that will return multiple values instead of one value – that is, getValues:

```
export class SampleService {

  getValues(): Observable<String> {
    return of('Hello', 'Packt', 'Readers');
  }
}
```

The values will be emitted one by one, in the aforementioned order. The test, when using the assert and subscribe pattern, will look like this:

```
it('should return values in the right order', (done) => {
  const expectedValues = ['Hello', 'Packt', 'Readers'];
  let index = 0;
  service.getValues().subscribe(result => {
    expect(result).toBe(expectedValues[index]);
    index++;
    done();
  });
});
```

In the preceding code, we created an array that represents the expected values in order and then simply subscribed to the `getValues` method and compared the emitted values with the expected value using a counter. After finishing, we called the `done()` callback.

Instead of the counter, we can use the `toArray` operator of RxJS, which will put the values that have been emitted in an array and then compare the resulting array with the expected array we defined, as follows:

```
it('should return values in the right order', (done) => {
  const expectedValues = ['Hello', 'Packt', 'Readers'];
  service.getValues().pipe(toArray()).subscribe(result => {
    expect(result).toEqual(expectedValues);
    done();
  });
});
```

Well, this is working fine and `ng test` will pass. But in both ways, even though we are dealing with a simple stream, we were forced to add some logic (in the first example, we added a counter, while in the second one, we used the `toArray` operator). This boils the tests and adds some unnecessary testing logic.

Now, let's take the previous example one step further and make it more complicated:

```
getRecurrentValues(): Observable<String> {
  return timer(0, 5000).pipe(
    take(3),
    switchMap((result) => of('Hello', 'Packt', 'Readers'))
  )
```

We are using the RxJS `timer` in this method to emit a value every 5 seconds. Since `timer` produces an endless stream, we call the `take` operator to return the first three emissions and complete them. Then, for every emission, we use the `switchMap` operator to return an observable that emits three values consecutively. This is tricky, right? If we use the subscribe and assert pattern here, the tests would be very complicated and may take a lot of time, depending on the value that's passed to `timer`. The unit tests should not take as much time; they should be fast and reliable. In this case, having a virtual time can be beneficial.

So, in a nutshell, the subscribe and assert pattern is a valid and easy technique that most developers adopt. However, it has some drawbacks that I pointed out throughout this section to be aware of, namely the following:

- We need to remember to call the done callback in asynchronous tests; otherwise, the tests will return invalid results.

- In some scenarios, we end up with boiled tests and unwanted testing logic.

- Timed observables are very complicated to test.

Now, let's explore another approach for testing observables: marble testing with RxJS testing utilities.

Learning about the marble testing pattern

Marble diagrams are very useful for visualizing observable execution. We learned about marble diagrams in *Chapter 1, The Power of the Reactive Paradigm*, and we've used them in almost all the reactive patterns we've implemented in this book. At this point, I think you are very familiar with marble diagrams. They are simple to understand and delightful to read. So, why not also use them in code? What you will be surprised to know is that RxJS introduced marble testing as an intuitive and clean way to test observables.

Let's discover what marble testing is about. We will start by explaining the syntax in the next section and then learn how we can write marble tests in our code.

Understanding the syntax

To understand the syntax, we should know about the following semantics:

Character	Meaning
' '	This represents a special character that will not be interpreted. It can be used to align your marble string.
'-'	This represents a frame of virtual time passing.
'|'	This represents the completion of an observable.
[a-z]	This represents a value that is emitted by an observable. It is an alphanumeric character.
'#'	This represents an error.
'()'	This represents a group of events that are occurring in the same frame. It can be used to group values emitted, errors, and completion.
'^'	This represents the subscription point and will only be used when you're dealing with hot observables.
[0-9]+[ms|s|m]	This represents the time progression. This allows you to progress virtual time by a specific amount. It's a number, followed by a time unit in milliseconds (ms), seconds (s), or minutes (m) without any space between them.

This is the basic syntax. Let's look at some examples to practice the syntax:

- `---`: This represents an observable that never emits.
- `-x--y--z|`: This represents an observable that emits x on the first frame, y on the fourth, and z on the seventh. After emitting z, the observable completes.
- `--xy--#`: This represents an observable that emits x on frame two, y on frame three, and an error on frame six.
- `-x^(yz)--|`: This is a hot observable that emits x before the subscription.

You've got the idea, right? Now, let's learn how to implement marble tests in our code.

Implementing marble tests

There are different packages out there that can help you write marble tests. The most well known are `jasmine-marbles`, `jest-marbles`, and `rxjs-marbles`. However, RxJS provides testing utilities out of the box and all the libraries are just wrappers around the RxJS testing utilities. I recommend working with the RxJS utilities for the following reasons:

- You don't have to include a third-party dependency.

- You stay up to date with the core implementation.

- You stay up to date with the latest features.

The API that's provided for testing in RxJS is based on `TestScheduler`. `TestScheduler` has a `run` method that has the following signature:

```
run<T>(callback: (helpers: RunHelpers) => T): T;
```

It takes `callback` as a parameter, which accepts a parameter of the `RunHelpers` type.

It gives us all the helper methods we need for marble testing. The interface contains the following properties:

```
export interface RunHelpers {
cold: typeof TestScheduler.prototype.
  createColdObservable;
hot: typeof TestScheduler.prototype.
  createHotObservable;
flush: typeof TestScheduler.prototype.flush;
expectObservable: typeof TestScheduler.
  prototype.expectObservable;
expectSubscriptions: typeof TestScheduler.
  prototype.expectSubscriptions;
}
```

Let's break down these properties one by one:

- `cold`: This produces a cold observable based on a given marble diagram. This is the signature of the method:

```
/**
     * @param marbles A diagram in the marble DSL.
        Letters map to keys in `values` if provided.
```

```
 * @param values Values to use for the letters in
   `marbles`. If omitted, the letters themselves
   are used.
 * @param error The error to use for the `#`
   marble (if present).
 */
createColdObservable<T = string>(marbles: string,
values?: {
      [marble: string]: T;
   }, error?: any): ColdObservable<T>;
```

- hot: This produces a hot observable based on a given marble diagram. This is the signature of the method:

```
/**
 * @param marbles A diagram in the marble DSL.
   Letters map to keys in `values` if provided.
 * @param values Values to use for the letters in
   `marbles`. If omitted, the letters themselves
   are used.
 * @param error The error to use for the `#`
   marble (if present).
 */
createHotObservable<T = string>(marbles: string, values?:
{
      [marble: string]: T;
   }, error?: any): HotObservable<T>;
```

When you're creating a hot observable, you can use ^ to point out the first frame.

- flush: This starts a virtual time. It's only needed if you use helpers outside the run callback or if you want to flush more than once.

- expectObservable: This asserts that an observable matches a marble diagram.

- expectSubscriptions: This asserts that an observable matches the expected subscriptions.

Now, let's go back to our example and see how we can implement marble testing for the `getValues` method:

```
export class SampleService {

  getValues(): Observable<String> {
    return of('Hello', 'Packt', 'Readers');
  }
}
```

The steps for writing the marble testing implementation pattern are simple:

1. Import `TestScheduler` from `rxjs/testing`:

    ```
    import { TestScheduler } from 'rxjs/testing';
    ```

2. In the `beforeEach` statement, inject `SampleService`. Then, instantiate `TestScheduler` and pass an `assertDeepEqual` function that tells `TestScheduler` how to compare values:

    ```
    import { TestScheduler } from 'rxjs/testing';
    describe('Service: SampleService, () => {
      let scheduler : TestScheduler;
      let service: SampleService;

      beforeEach(() => {
        service = TestBed.inject(SampleService);
        scheduler = new TestScheduler((actual, expected)
        => {
        expect(actual).toEqual(expected);
      });
    ```

    The methods that are used to compare values depend on your testing framework.

3. Use `TestScheduler` to test your stream by calling the `run` method and passing a callback to it. Remember that the callback needs to accept `RunHelpers` as the first parameter:

    ```
    it('should return values in the right order', () => {
      scheduler.run((helpers) => {
      });
    });
    ```

Instead of using the helpers directly, it is useful to destructure the helpers into variables and use them directly to implement the marble tests. We will be destructuring the expectObservable variable as we will use it to assert that the observable matches the marble diagram, as follows:

```
it('should return values in the right order', () => {
  scheduler.run(({expectObservable}) => {
  });
});
```

4. The last step is declaring the expected marble and values and performing the expectation, as follows:

```
it('should return values in the right order', () => {
  scheduler.run(({expectObservable}) => {
    const expectedMarble = '(abc|)' ;
    const expectedValues = {a:'Hello', b:'Packt',
      c:'Readers'};
    expectObservable(service.getValues()).toBe(
    expectedMarble, expectedValues)
  });
});
```

The expectedMarble constant represents the marble diagram. Since the getValues method returns three values consecutively, we used parentheses to group the a, b, and c emissions; the stream then completes, so we use the | character.

The expectedValues constant represents the values of the a, b, and c characters that we put in expectedMarble. It represents 'Hello', 'Packt', and 'Readers' consecutively, which are nothing but the values that are emitted by the observable that we want to test.

The last instruction is the expectation; we should provide the expected result that our methods should return. Here, we must use expectObservable, which takes the observable we want to test as a parameter and matches it with expectedMarble and expectedValues.

That's it. Let's have a look at the complete test setup:

```
describe('SampleService marble tests', () => {
  let scheduler : TestScheduler ;
```

```
let service: SampleService;


beforeEach(() => {
  service = TestBed.inject(SampleService);
  scheduler = new TestScheduler((actual, expected) => {
  expect(actual).toEqual(expected);
});
});


it('should return values in the right order', () => {
  scheduler.run(({expectObservable}) => {
   const expectedMarble = '(abc|)' ;
   const expectedValues = {a:'Hello', b:'Packt',
     c:'Readers'};
   expectObservable(service.getValues()).toBe(
     expectedMarble, expectedValues)
  });
});
});
```

When you run ng test, this test will pass. If you put wrong values in expectedValues, you will see the test failing:

```
Chrome 95.0.4638.69 (Windows 10) SampleService marble tests should return values in the right order FAILED
       Error: Expected $[0].notification.value = 'Hello' to equal 'Hello22'.
          at <Jasmine>
          at TestScheduler.assertDeepEqual (src/app/core/services/shared-data.service.spec.ts:43:18)
          at node_modules/rxjs/_esm2015/internal/testing/TestScheduler.js:110:1
          at Array.filter (<anonymous>)
Chrome 95.0.4638.69 (Windows 10): Executed 4 of 10 (1 FAILED) (skipped 6) (0.073 secs / 0.043 secs)
TOTAL: 1 FAILED, 3 SUCCESS
```

Figure 13.2 - ng test failing

Well, this is cleaner than the implementation that used the subscribe and assert pattern.

Now, let's look at a more difficult example – the timed observable that was complicated to implement using the subscribe and assert pattern:

```
getRecurrentValues(): Observable<String> {
  return timer(0, 5000).pipe(
    take(3),
    switchMap((result) => of('Hello', 'Packt',
```

```
            'Readers'))
    )
  }
```

The cool feature of `TestScheduler` that can help us here is *virtual time*. It allows us to test asynchronous streams synchronously by virtualizing time and ensuring that the correct items are emitted at the correct time. Thanks to the time progression syntax, we can advance virtual time by milliseconds (ms), seconds (s), or even minutes (m). This is extremely useful in the case of timed observables. Let's consider the following marble diagram:

e 999ms (fg) 996ms h 999ms (i|)';

Here, the diagram indicates that e is emitted immediately. Then, after 1 second, f and g are emitted. 1 second later, h is emitted, after which i is emitted, and the stream finally completes.

Why `999` and `996`? We're using `999` because e takes 1 ms to emit and `996` because the characters in the (`fg`) group take 1 ms each.

With all this in mind, the marble tests of `getRecurrentValues` will look like this:

```
    const expectedMarble = '(abc) 4995ms (abc) 4995ms
    (abc|)' ;
```

The group of values (`abc`) are emitted every 5 seconds or 5,000 ms and since the characters are counted inside the group, we put `4995ms`. So, the whole test case will look as follows:

```
it('should return values in the right time', () => {
  scheduler.run(({expectObservable}) => {
    const expectedMarble = '(abc) 4995ms (abc) 4995ms
    (abc|)' ;
    const expectedValues = {a:'Hello', b:'Packt',
      c:'Readers'};
    expectObservable(service.getRecurrentValues()).toBe(
      expectedMarble, expectedValues)
  });
});
```

That's how we resolved the test of a timed observable using marble tests.

Marble testing is extremely powerful and helpful. It allows you to test a very high level of detail and complicated things such as concurrency and timed observables. It also makes your tests cleaner. However, it requires you to learn a new syntax and it is not recommended for testing business logic. Marble testing was designed for testing operators with arbitrary time.

> **Note**
>
> For more details about marble testing, you can check out the official docs at `https://rxjs.dev/guide/testing/marble-testing`.

Now, let's highlight a very common pattern for testing business logic.

Highlighting testing streams using HttpClientTestingModule

Observables that are returned from the HTTP client are frequently used in our Angular code. How can we test those streams? Let's look at the pattern we can use to test those observables. We will consider the following method inside `RecipeService`:

```
saveRecipe(formValue: Recipe): Observable<Recipe> {
  return this.http.post<Recipe>(
    `${BASE_PATH}/recipes/save`, formValue);
}
```

The `saveRecipe` method issues an HTTP request. There is a very useful API that can be used in this case: `HttpClientTestingModule`. This API allows us to test HTTP methods that use the HTTP client. It also allows us to easily mock HTTP requests by providing the `HttpTestingController` service. In short, it enables us to mock requests instead of making real API requests to our API backend when testing.

Let's look at the pattern's steps:

1. Before you can use `HttpClientTestingModule` and its `HttpTestingController` service, you need to import and provide them in your `TestBed`, alongside the service we are testing. In our case, this is `RecipesService`.

2. Then, we must inject `HttpTestingController` and `RecipesService` and provide a shared instance of each to use in our tests:

```
import { TestBed } from '@angular/core/testing';
import { HttpClientTestingModule, HttpTestingController }
from '@angular/common/http/testing';
import { RecipesService } from './recipes.service';

describe('RecipesService', () => {

  let service: RecipesService;
  let httpTestingController: HttpTestingController;

  beforeEach(() => {
    TestBed.configureTestingModule({
      imports: [HttpClientTestingModule],
      providers: [RecipesService]
    });
    httpTestingController =
     TestBed.inject(HttpTestingController)
    service = TestBed.inject(RecipesService)
  });
});
```

3. Then, we must implement the test case of saving the recipe. Let's mock `saveRecipe`, as follows:

```
it('should save recipe from API', () => {
  const recipeToSave : Recipe= {
    "id": 9,
    "title": "Lemon cake",
    "prepTime": "10",
    "cookingTime": "35",
    "rating": 3,
    "imageUrl": "lemon-cake.jpg"

  }
  const subscription =
```

```
service.saveRecipe(recipeToSave)
  .subscribe(_recipe => {
    expect(recipeToSave).toEqual(_recipe, 'should
    check mock data')
  });
const req = httpTestingController.expectOne(
  `/api/recipes/save`);
req.flush(recipeToSave);
subscription.unsubscribe();
});
```

Let's break down what is happening in this code. Here, we created a constant called `recipeToSave` that represents a mocked recipe that we will post to the server to be saved. Then, we subscribed to the `saveRecipe` method and passed `recipeToSave` to it as a parameter. Inside the subscription, we defined our expectations. Then, we called the `expectOne` method, which expects a single request that's been made to match a given URL (in our case, `/api/recipes/save`) and returns mock data using the `flush` method, which resolves the request by returning a mocked body. Finally, we released the subscription.

4. Finally, we must add an `afterEach()` block, in which we run the `verify` method of our controller, as follows:

```
afterEach(() => {
  httpTestingController.verify();
});
```

This ensures that no request is outstanding. And that's it! This is the pattern for testing methods that issue HTTP requests.

`HttpClientTestingModule` is very useful in this use case. For more details about `HttpClientTestingModule`, please refer to `https://angular.io/api/common/http/testing/HttpClientTestingModule`.

Summary

There is no perfect solution for every use case. In this chapter, I tried to show you the common solutions that are available in RxJS and Angular for testing observables. And you can choose the solution that fits your project best. First, we learned about the subscribe and assert pattern, as well as its advantages and drawbacks.

Then, we learned about the marble testing pattern, its syntax, features, advantages, and drawbacks. We studied a basic example and an example that uses virtual time to test timed observables.

Finally, we learned about a pattern we can use to test streams that are returned from the HTTP client. Now that you know about the common techniques that are available in the Angular/RxJS ecosystem (without having to add a third-party library), it is up to you to pick the right technique for the right use case.

This was our last pattern and our journey into reactive patterns has come to an end. I tried to highlight the most-used reactive patterns that solve a lot of recurrent use cases in web applications. You can use them immediately in your current projects, adapt them to your needs, or get inspired to create your own reactive pattern. I think that you should have noticed by now that this book is not only about the patterns but also about the reactive approach and how to switch your mindset from imperative to reactive thinking. That's why I always highlighted in all the chapters the classic pattern before the reactive one to enable a smooth transition.

Index

Subscribe to our online digital library for full access to over 7,000 books and videos, as well as industry leading tools to help you plan your personal development and advance your career. For more information, please visit our website.

Why subscribe?

- Spend less time learning and more time coding with practical eBooks and Videos from over 4,000 industry professionals

- Improve your learning with Skill Plans built especially for you

- Get a free eBook or video every month

- Fully searchable for easy access to vital information

- Copy and paste, print, and bookmark content

Did you know that Packt offers eBook versions of every book published, with PDF and ePub files available? You can upgrade to the eBook version at packt.com and as a print book customer, you are entitled to a discount on the eBook copy. Get in touch with us at customercare@packtpub.com for more details.

At www.packt.com, you can also read a collection of free technical articles, sign up for a range of free newsletters, and receive exclusive discounts and offers on Packt books and eBooks.

Other Books You May Enjoy

If you enjoyed this book, you may be interested in these other books by Packt:

Learning Angular - Third Edition

Aristeidis Bampakos , Pablo Deeleman

ISBN: 978-1-83921-066-2

- Use the Angular CLI to scaffold, build, and deploy a new Angular application
- Build components, the basic building blocks of an Angular application
- Discover techniques to make Angular components interact with each other
- Understand the different types of templates supported by Angular
- Create HTTP data services to access APIs and provide data to components

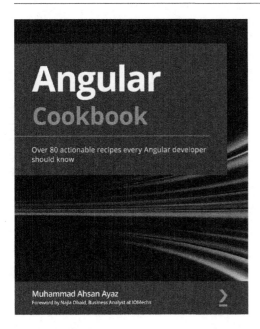

Angular Cookbook

Muhammad Ahsan Ayaz

ISBN: 978-1-83898-943-9

- Gain a better understanding of how components, services, and directives work in Angular
- Understand how to create Progressive Web Apps using Angular from scratch
- Build rich animations and add them to your Angular apps
- Manage your app's data reactivity using RxJS
- Implement state management for your Angular apps with NgRx

Packt is searching for authors like you

If you're interested in becoming an author for Packt, please visit `authors.packtpub.com` and apply today. We have worked with thousands of developers and tech professionals, just like you, to help them share their insight with the global tech community. You can make a general application, apply for a specific hot topic that we are recruiting an author for, or submit your own idea.

Share Your Thoughts

Now you've finished *Reactive Patterns with RxJS for Angular*, we'd love to hear your thoughts! Scan the QR code below to go straight to the Amazon review page for this book and share your feedback or leave a review on the site that you purchased it from.

https://packt.link/r/1801811512

Your review is important to us and the tech community and will help us make sure we're delivering excellent quality content.

Printed in Great Britain
by Amazon

22731394R00126